I0192816

"The New Wave Energy Awareness" original
copyright © 2013
ISBN – 13: 978-0615888200
ISBN – 10: 0615888208

DISCLAIMER

The information in this book is intended to help readers become aware of the possibilities connected to energy healing for themselves, friends and loved ones. It is not intended to be a substitute for treatment by or advice and care of a professional health-care provider.

♥

DEDICATION

This book is dedicated to my husband, Bob, the love of my life. He has never criticized or judged me in any way during our many years together. He has stood by me with patience and understanding as we expand our consciousness and energy awareness together. I am so grateful for all we have shared and continue to share on our life's journey together. Thank you Bob, for being you, all you have shared with me over the years and the deep love that is beyond words.

CONTENTS

ROLE PLAYING

CHANGE

SUMMARY

TOOLS
Colour Energy
Sound
Aromatherapy
Hypnotherapy
Energy Testing

RESOURCES
Movies
Speakers/Interviewers
Healing Modalities
Books
Body Healing
Scientific Data
Quantum Healers
Remote Healers

INTRODUCTION

My purpose in writing this book was to help facilitate a better understanding of energy healing, awareness and to also expand energy consciousness. Everything is energy, always will be and this includes our thoughts, actions and experiences.

Some of the information, concepts and explanations may seem simple but I can assure you that when energy awareness expands, the quality of life, choices, relationships and experiences will also change and expand. This opens up a whole new paradigm collectively and individually to possibilities and potentials.

For those who aren't aware, there is a large mass of energy awareness taking place across the globe. It's a time in history when people are searching for answers, truth, questioning the very foundation of their beliefs and the existing realities as we know them.

The Information Age and new technology has given us the ability to be able to communicate across the globe, access an endless loop of information and data at any given moment in time. With this movement also came overwhelming amounts of information, marketing, data and constant outside stimulation.

Being stuck or trapped in outside stimulation and marketing can keep us always searching outside ourselves for answers. Being controlled by outside sources can lead to living a very limited, superficial life with a total lack of self-awareness.

Nobody really knows what the future will bring or what will follow the Information Age. It is my hope that energy awareness becomes a priority for our children and all of humanity. After many hours of researching, studying and working with people, I have found there is a desperate need to help people of all ages have more self-confidence, self-esteem and self-love on a continuous basis, from birth to transition from Earth.

Another great need for mankind at this time is education on energy awareness connected to emotions. Many of us were never taught what to do with emotions and we are now dealing with buried emotions and emotional trauma that was never healed.

This book was written to help people understand that beliefs and emotions are at the base of everything we experience, because they are intertwined and interconnected in our energetic beings. When beliefs and emotions from experiences, get stuck, trapped or buried within our being, they can remain there for years, creating states of hurt, pain, and struggle, which can lead to suffering, whether that is in our health, relationship's with ourselves, others or any other area of our life.

Another area that I believe needs to be expanded, which would be of great value to all, teaching people and especially children how to use their skills, imagination and ability to create. Create it in the mind and thus you make it real.

A very large percentage of the population has become trapped in doing steps one through ten, in the right way in order to survive. Living in survival mode and not being able to see beyond that, not only limits you, but is very unhealthy on many different levels and this is creating many unhappy people. We are creative beings that need to create for our well-being.

Join me and millions of others in our search of truth, individually and collectively, as we expand our consciousness, raise our energy frequencies and claim the greatness we truly were meant to be. You will find some of the key components in the pages that follow, which can help you on your quest for truth and self-awareness.

STACKING
BLOCKS

Experiences come and go like jelly beans, different flavors, colors, shapes, sizes and packaging. Experiences fill your daily life, individually and collectively, would you not agree? So at any given moment in time, you are experiencing life, is that not so? Can you go through life without experiencing it? It's important that you understand this concept because this is where your power resides.

Would you agree that whether you are waking up, sleeping, having a cup of coffee, brushing your teeth, having an argument or climbing a mountain, you are experiencing life? You might say "This is a no brainer", but you will understand the importance of this as we continue. The reference to stacking blocks is about stacking experiences.

Let's take a look at some examples of starting a day (stacking blocks).

> Did you start your day with the experience of a cup of coffee, while watching a beautiful sunrise?

Did you experience getting up on the wrong side of the bed?

Did you experience waking up happy and filled with abundant energy?

These are all experiences, with very different emotions to start your day. Sounds to simple right? Let's take a look at the person that started their day with a cup of coffee and the beautiful sunrise. What emotions can you find in the above experience? Could there be peace, serenity and harmony? Now how about the person that got up on the wrong side of the bed? What emotions can you find in this experience? Would you find anger, frustration or aggression? Last, let's take a look at the person waking up happy, filled with an abundance of energy. Could there be joy, happiness and laughter attached to this experience?

These are all examples which illustrate that life is full of many different experiences with their attached emotions. If you understand that life is about experiences with attached emotions, you begin to understand life isn't happening to you, you are creating your own experiences. How can this help me?

First, it will help you look at life differently, so you can start creating your life and experiences.

Second, it helps with not taking experiences so personally, hanging onto them for dear life.

Third, you begin to realize you are a powerful, unlimited being with a gift to choose your experiences which will help set you free.

Fourth, we must **stop claiming what we don't want!**

A word of caution; **choosing your experiences needs to come from the heart**, not the intellect, in order for your life to flow with ease and grace. How do I do that? This simple technique is very powerful and is a key.

~ Quiet your mind by placing your hand on your heart.

~ Breathe in and out through your heart space.

~ Focus your attention on your heart as long as possible.

~ It's best to start with simple questions.

~ What would I like to experience? Would I like to experience this or that?"

~ The power of intention and attention is a must in order to access your truth.

~ Now notice any feelings, sensations, heaviness, lightness, symbols that arise or anything else. Just notice what you notice, no judgment.

~ It is OK if you get nothing at first because your mind still quiets with focused attention. Be patient and consistent.

~ You may need to learn some kind of relaxation technique or learn to meditate to quiet the busy chatter in the mind.

~ Here is where you can practice becoming familiar with the true you, your truth and the power that resides within.

This simple technique can be used anytime and anywhere and will return you to your heart center. The heart never lies and only gives you what is in your best interest. It is said that your heart is 5,000 times more powerful than your intellect because the intellect and mind have way too many stories attached. Stories and the past will only get in the way of finding your truth. Many people are trapped in their head and being controlled by their mind.

Did you notice when you did the exercise above, the chatter in the mind quiets as you focus on your heart? This powerful technique will take some time and practice but your rewards will be beyond any words or descriptions. Be patient, your answers will come in time and in case you didn't know it, there is an average of about 21-30 days practice that is required to integrate a new behavior. Accessing your truth through your heart is your life gps, your gift and nothing outside yourself will ever change that. No guru, friend or family member can ever know what is best for you, only you!

The power of focused attention (intention) can move mountains and is usually a hidden emotion behind everything consciously or unconsciously. Wayne Dyers' book "The Power of Intention" will help you understand in depth, the power of intention. "You can't solve a problem from the same space it was created".

Here is another technique that can expand your energy awareness and experiences.

~ **Does (whatever you chose) feel
light or heavy. If it feels heavy in
your heart, that is a no and if it
feels light, that is a yes.**

We already know this and experience it, but
have too many distractions to pay attention.
It's a guiding light through the emotional
maze of experiencing life. Here are some
examples that may help you.

You walk into someone's home, they
just had a fight and you feel the
confusion, stress, chaos and drama.

Can you find the many different emotions in
this experience? Do they feel light or heavy?
So now take a moment to become familiar
with what feels light or heavy.

How about when you first learned to
ride a bike or drive a car?

How about that orange that smells so
good?

How about that person that drives you crazy?

How about listening to the news?

How about that movie you recently saw?

I think you will find that fear, anger, guilt, shame, hate and similar emotions feel heavy and that lighter energy frequencies would be joy, love and laughter. You can use this technique with any person, place, thing, anytime and anywhere. Awareness is your key.

Now let's visit someone's beautiful home that has lots of windows, very spacious, beautiful decor, happy music playing, it's very colorful and everyone in that home seems to be happy and radiate joyfulness.

These are all experiences that are filled with emotions from our emotional maze. Which one would you choose? Most people are attracted to people that are happy and radiate power with grace.

How can this help you in your life? If you make choices of experiences from within your heart that empower you and feel good, you radiate that energy and attract more of it back to you. Like attracts like, this is just one of the universal laws of energy.

By now I hope you understand life is experience, after experience, stacked like blocks, on top of one another. At any given time you have a choice of what you would like to experience. Do I want to play or don't I? This applies to all areas of your life including relationships, money and health. Your power lies in your free will of choice.

Would you like to change some choices that are draining your energy, stressing you out and disempowering you? You can change your mind, you are allowed, and it's OK!

Could it be that friend who has stopped being a friend?

Could it be a job that makes you feel bad?

Could it be a choice of poverty, money is bad or evil?

You have the power and you are an unlimited being regardless of what you are experiencing now. Unlimited choices are like jelly beans, empower yourself with the best flavors and most colorful experiences you can.

Does this mean you won't experience dis-empowering experiences? No, depending on what you have learned by the experience (we are all here to learn and evolve), how long you want to stay trapped in the experience, how much emotional investment and attachment you have and when you decide enough is enough. You can then release the experience and move on.

There is a saying "How can you expect to change when you keep trying to do the same thing over and over, expecting different results". Realize it's only an experience that you are trapped in and that you have the freedom of choice.

Some experiences have been trapped for a lifetime and no matter how hard you try to let go of them, they just seem like they are stuck forever.

As you read on, you will understand why these experiences get trapped or maybe you already know, but need some help with methods or tools to get unstuck from dis-empowering experiences.

"Who is creating my experiences?"

TREASURE BOX

Did you know that you have a treasure box filled with your very own treasures? Your treasure box is filled with many different emotions that you can choose to feel at any given moment.

Life is all about choices, experiences (jelly beans) and a treasure box filled with emotions that can ultimately give us the power to choose the best for ourselves. Is there anyone or anything outside yourself that can know what truly resonates with your heart? Know thyself, where have you heard those words? Maybe we can learn from others with similar experiences and that will give us new insight on how to handle a current experience but ultimately, we still have to choose.

Our journey through the school of life as an emotional human being is composed of choices, experiences and emotions, welcome to planet Earth. Can you have an experience without emotions? Can you have emotions without experiences?

For those that believe experiences happen to them and we don't create our experiences, it doesn't matter (right, wrong, good or bad), we still have to go through the experience. We can decide whether we want to learn from the experience, release it with ease and grace or hold onto it emotionally in a state of constant struggle, hurt, pain and suffering. Life was never meant to be a struggle. We create struggle by holding onto emotional experiences for dear life in the mind and body connection.

Finding your truth will take you on your own personal journey through the emotional maze. The emotional maze consists of finding the dominating emotional attachment to whichever experience you are holding onto. Some questions you might ask yourself, are these emotions causing suffering, depleted energy, creating stress or making me sick? Another question might be is this experience causing pain or pleasure and is it possible for anyone to do this for me?

At this point, it's important to decide, are my emotions and experiences controlling me and my life or who is driving the bus? Let's take a look at a simple example.

> In the younger years there was a child that went to school where the kids would always make fun of the way the child dressed (experience). As this child grew up, the child decided it was really important to dress a certain way. They didn't fit in, something was wrong with them. The child carried that experience for a lifetime.

Can you find all the emotions in this emotional maze experience? Could there be self-consciousness, feelings of not fitting in, fear of rejection, fear of being made fun of, embarrassment, humiliation, hurt or anger? Chances are that this child is still living with this experience well into adulthood and several emotions became energetically trapped in the body and mind.

Depending on the child, the experience above can go many different directions and become emotionally stuck. The experience is the seed that was planted that begins to grow and develop a life of its own. Examples of this might be;

(Child A) Becomes shy, withdrawn and feels they will never fit in. Not fitting in starts to grow into all areas of their life and this person doesn't understand why they don't fit in. They are emitting that energy, even though they may not be aware consciously of it (remember like attracts like).

(Child B) Becomes angry and decides they don't care what anyone thinks. Maybe this child will become defiant, bitter and want revenge.

(Child C) Becomes self-conscious and as they grow older, may experience compulsive buying and shopping habits. All the new clothes in the world will not make them feel better.

(Child D) Becomes a child that just goes through life not really doing the things they would like to do, living in fear of humiliation or feeling that they are not good enough.

Simple examples, but this experience can have very profound effects throughout their life. There are thousands of simple experiences that can grow into monsters. Have you ever noticed that your perception of an experience is quite different from others, even other family members, raised in the same household?

Why do we get stuck in an experience? Once we have the experience and add emotions, the experience then becomes powerful. The more senses included (sight, hearing, feelings, olfactory, touch), the more powerful that experience becomes (good, bad, right or wrong) it doesn't matter, the results speak for themselves. There are numerous examples of emotional experiences that can get trapped energetically in our beings.

Everything is energy, always will be and this includes thoughts and emotions.

Energetically, some experiences just pass through our energy field because there is no personal or emotional attachment, while others stay for a lifetime. Some experiences are passed on from parents, ancestors, past lives, friends, family, socially, school, media, global consciousness and numerous other sources. Some common examples I have found in my research and sessions are:

> It's amazing how many people don't consider themselves to be good people in their hearts, even those who always do good things for others and give their heart to others. There are several different beliefs connected to this and it can also stem from childhood experiences such as, good or bad, girl or boy.

Oldest siblings often can feel resentment, burdened and angry from being responsible for helping to raise their siblings. Sometimes, they choose not to have children because of this experience.

Many feel like they continuously have to prove themselves to others, family, friends, employers and parents (even if the parents have passed on).

Not having a sense of belonging, fitting in, fear of rejection or feeling left out is common. These are all huge issues and blocks that can lead to destructive trapped energy.

Many lack self-confidence, self-esteem and/or self-worth, not feeling loved, wanted or needed.

Money issues connected to childhood experiences, carried into adulthood.

Many are unaware they are experiencing empathetic, stuck energy in their being that doesn't belong to them.

People pleasers that consistently do anything and everything to please others, friends and family, even if that means self-destruction.

Many carry trapped, stored, stuck anger and rage that has never been dealt with. The anger layers until it becomes rage.

Favoritism is another common energy issue from childhood which became stuck and trapped energetically in the mind and body.

There are many that believe they will never be able to do enough or be enough, no matter how hard they try. Feeling alone without support, having to do everything themselves.

Fear is running rampant and emotionally attached to several issues.

Indecision, confusion, what do I really want? What is my purpose? I don't know what to do, nothing is working.

Not understanding why they are feeling stuck, trapped, held back or blocked.

Trapped and stuck in dead-end relationships, family issues, or feeling financially limited with several work issues.

Trapped or stuck in playing the role of victim or playing the blame game.

The list goes on and on, there are no road maps outside our own treasure box of emotions that can guide us through the emotional maze. There are numerous healers, methods and tools available to help us on our journey.

Have you ever noticed when you are looking with the power of intention, you meet a special person that can help, hear a song that has the answer or see a billboard that captures your attention?

The answers usually come from unexpected sources and there are signs or symbols all around us but we get side tracked. The answers are usually very simple, so simple we often overlook them. Taking responsibility for our lives, our creations with powerful intention takes strength and courage.

If we bury our emotions, sooner or later those buried emotions will affect our life in all areas, whether that is relationships, jobs or business. Using alcohol and drugs (legal or illegal) can be another way of burying emotions.

Most of us were never taught what to do with emotions, how to let them pass through without becoming attached, not reliving them time and time again, or passing them on through generations. In the end, this only creates suffering and blocks our ability to create what we would truly like to experience.

The law of attraction is just that, whatever we are sending out in our thoughts, feelings or emotionally is what we will receive back in experiences (good or bad). If we take time to honestly look within and around ourselves, we know what is being attracted to us. If you're sending out less than desirable emotions, are you ready to make changes and choices to attract what you do want to experience? We can't be in two places at the same time. Some examples of this might be.

Wanting to experience abundance and spending the majority of time in lack.

Hating a relationship experience you're currently in, while wanting a new empowering relationship.

Hating your job and creating something you would rather experience.

It's not possible to find more rewarding, fulfilling relationships and be trapped in gossiping, criticizing, judgment and drama.

Stuck and trapped in a life filled with chaos, trauma and dysfunction but at the same time expecting to experience peace.

Expectations of wanting to experience more love, joy and prosperity with life flowing easily and with grace, while living in a continual stressed out state.

It doesn't matter where we start, we need to start somewhere, otherwise, we will be nowhere. Sometimes baby steps can change our life quickly. The following common beliefs might work for a while but will never be satisfying in the long run.

I will be happy when I have my own house.

I will be satisfied when I have the job I want.

I will feel loved when I meet my soul mate.

If only so and so would change my life would be better.

If I only had more money, my life would be better.

In conclusion, we are emotional beings. We want to experience many things on our journey, which is a good thing. When we get stuck, there is no creation taking place to experience or, we lose our zest for life and all the higher frequencies of joy, love, laughter and abundance disappear.

If this happens, the experience can turn into emotionally sinking deeper and deeper into despair, depression, anger, sadness, hurt, pain and suffering, which can lead to creating more of the same. Negative experiences connected to emotions will keep going around and around, creating the inability to see out of the emotional maze.

Now let's take a look at the endless possibilities of creating our own personal story.

"Emotions are natural, like floating clouds, not meant to be held onto or contained, controlling our lives."

THE
STORY

We can now create our very own personal story by combining the jelly beans (experiences) with emotions from our treasure box.

This simple concept is the core of our journey. We are continually experiencing life while building and creating our story from day to day. This is where the concept comes from, it's not the destination that's important, it's the journey.

Another way you can understand the creation process is by looking at your life as a movie. In a lot of ways our life is no different than a movie. We create characters, colors, pictures; add drama and emotions to our experience, creating our life story. There are sad, happy, funny movies, horror shows, reality shows and many other examples of experiences made into movies to ignite our senses and emotions. It's all part of the natural human experience process.

Often times we get emotionally stuck in our story or maybe even in other peoples stories, instead of creating our own. Maybe we even get trapped into believing we can fix other peoples stories.

Stories exist no matter where you go or what you do. We each have our own story, some are worse than others. Stories can motivate us, uplift our spirits, create fear, and some make us laugh, while still others reach our hearts. No matter how you look at it, there are emotions connected to the stories of our lives.

When we realize and become aware we are emotional beings in a human body, experiencing life, we can then realize we are not our story. This helps us to begin taking conscious control of creating the story we would like to experience, rather than being trapped in a story that is not serving us, doesn't stimulate us and keeps us energetically stagnant and stuck. It is our natural ability to create, we are creative beings.

Somehow the word create, took on different meanings for different people, consciously and unconsciously. Some believe you can only create if you are a painter or artist. Others believe they are not a creative person and some people became afraid to create for various reasons. Still others feel like they don't know how and become stuck going nowhere, blowing in the wind, wherever life takes them. These are beliefs that are untrue because everything you see around you was created with thoughts, experiences and emotions. You were created, so how is it possible that you can't be a creative person. If you are creating a special meal, playing a guitar, reading a book, taking a nice hot bubble bath or watching a movie, you are creating and experiencing. It's never too late to start creating, no matter where you are now, no matter what age you are, if you believe you can create, you will. There are plenty of life stories that prove creation is possible, which can motivate us to take action. Taking time to listen or read some of these stories can lift up our spirits and help give us the courage or strength to move on.

Become the observer of your life, use the power of intention and begin taking an active part in your creation, while looking objectively at all areas of your story.

What parts or chapters of your story are you ready to re-create, change or is there a new chapter you would like to begin creating and experiencing? Remember, you aren't the experience, you are the creator and you have the ability and skills to create.

The most successful creators are the ones who are doing what they love while utilizing the creative process. One of the best things about creating your story, if you don't like it and it isn't flowing, you have the power to create a new one, and it's OK!!! We love to tell, hear and read stories, isn't that part of the life experience?

There are several reasons why we hold onto stories that don't serve us but the main ones are fear and security issues. Some people are experiencing losing their jobs, family and a multitude of other experiences all at the same time.

When asking different people from all walks of life who they are, most begin describing the many different roles they play in life, start naming titles and then they share their story. Like the movies, each person plays many different roles throughout their journey. We learn from all our different experiences, characters we play and if we become too emotionally attached to that, it can prevent us from expanding into new roles and experiences we would rather include in our life story.

A good example might be a school teacher that has been teaching for several years in the same school and the same area. Maybe they've outgrown the experience of being a school teacher but can't tell themselves to move on because of retirement issues or numerous other reasons. Letting go can be a very frightening experience. What if the teacher decided to expand into private tutoring with more freedom, what if this teacher could experience being a professor or what if this teacher wanted to pursue something completely different?

The movie "Flashdance" is a good example of working towards a dream while doing what's necessary to experience the dream. This movie portrays the emotional challenges hidden in the emotional maze that must be overcome for her to experience living the dream. The very popular movie "Dirty Dancing" touched the hearts of many as we watched them work through conquering their own personal fears.

Many different emotions will arise as we decide to pursue our dreams and sometimes we don't even know which emotions may be blocking us. The majority of the emotional blocks are hidden, stacked and layered because of life experiences.

Here is a simple example: wanting to be a pianist in a symphony (dream).

Let's say that they start with no money, piano or music classes to attend.

Positives:

Love to listen to piano music.

Read all the stories or books about favorite pianist.

Get excited every time while imagining playing the piano, even if you don't have a piano.

Love looking at the different styles of pianos.

Feels so good while listening to piano music, it lifts the spirit.

Negatives:

Never going to be possible to have the money that is needed to learn to play the piano or buy a piano. What's the use?

There is no way I will ever be good enough to play in a symphony.

My parents don't like piano music.

I'm afraid my friends will think that I'm really stupid.

My fingers aren't long enough and it will be too hard.

Above are two very different emotional experiences for making their dream a reality. Which one do you think will help you to succeed? Remember, you can't be in two places in your mind at the same time and create anything.

Let's take another example using a person that had a dream of being a farmer. This person's experience started with an idea and dream of buying some land, developing it, farming the land, building a home and as time progressed, his dream was fulfilled.

Maybe now he wants to buy more acreage or is completely content with what he now has.

Now, let's say this farmer had a bad year of weather which created some financial challenges. Will he choose to be innovative and creative? Maybe the farmer decides to diversify into producing ethanol, maybe he will create and rent some of his land for garden plots, maybe this farmer will start hay rides, barn dances or develop mazes in the wheat fields, or start green houses to supply food all year long to many.

Once again the possibilities of expansion are endless but if this farmer stays in the space of struggle, worry or financial hardship, that is what will be created, more of the same. Creating something new or different requires moving with the times of change (supply and demand).

Once I heard of a story where a man was losing his farm and the bank wouldn't lend him any money. He went to the community and sold shares in his land to community members. He saved the farm and was able to meet his financial obligations. It was a win, win for the man, his family and his community. How does it get any better than that?

Will there be times when we lose faith, feel it's not possible or wonder if it will ever happen? Absolutely! The most important thing at those moments is to become aware of those negative thoughts (like clouds passing through) and bring yourself back to the positive.

Use whatever you can to reignite the flame; read that success story again, listen to some piano music, play in the imagination, dance or anything else that will lift you up to a higher, lighter vibration.

The negative chatter in the mind is only trying to protect you. If you try to turn the chatter off, it will only get louder and create more of the same. Kind of like, don't think of a pink elephant. Did you think of the pink elephant? Acknowledge, feel and change the channel. You might also try some breathing exercise, counting backward to break the pattern that you are stuck in or try using relaxation techniques that can also help.

You can learn to quiet the chatter. The more you practice, the better you will get at not staying for long in those negative conversations in the mind. If you are into the past, it's all about experiences and emotional connections to the story. If you are into the future, there can be a certain amount of fear attached to the unknown. The best place to be is in the experience of what is happening in this moment (now).

Many people are trapped in the analytical mind experiencing boredom, just going through steps one through ten. Steps one through ten, done right and in the right order can really limit the imagination, our creative abilities and keep us stuck.

Have you ever had pie before dinner? Have you ever taken a different road to work? Have you ever done anything spontaneous? Simple little things can get energy moving. If you start moving out of procedures, patterns and habits into different ways of experiencing and new experiences, you can expand your consciousness rather than limit it by staying in the box, doing the same thing over and over, wanting change but not allowing yourself to experience it. Maybe that lunch with a new friend, in a different dining experience will create something you never thought possible.

Try making your story a little different each day and see what happens. Nothing shared here will work if you don't see and experience it for yourself.

If you just read about how to, never apply or try it in your own life, how can you decide what works for you? There are endless possibilities to create but if we get stuck in the structure, familiar or boxed in, we won't experience change, no matter how hard we try. We need structure but too much structure can cause being stuck in the mud.

Another place many people seem to be stuck, what do I want to do when I grow up, regardless of their age or profession. Is it possible to experience different characters and roles while being stuck in this old programing?

We have the power and ability to serve or create whatever we choose. It goes without saying, our choice should be something we love, enjoy doing or we will be creating struggle and swimming upstream. Any time any experience turns into constant struggle, there is something wrong, take a moment when you catch this happening, become the observer and either release it or take a different path.

Old programing taught us to pick a career and stay there for life. If you want to stay in the same career for life that is your personal choice but it's no longer set in concrete like it use to be. I'll be nobody unless (fill in the blank). Many of those opportunities have come and gone. Many are learning to use their skills, creating their own businesses and happier now than they have ever been.

I often tell people to watch out for titles as they are often very misleading. The doctor, lawyer, garbage man, plumber, retail clerk is just as important to all of us.

There is no one on this planet that is more important than you. We each have our own unique gifts and skills. Realizing your power lies beyond all the superficial titles and roles can help you break free of limiting beliefs, which can cause a tremendous amount of suffering and keep you stuck in a state of always trying to measure up.

Another common question is what am I doing here? Simple as it may sound, what if being here is only about experiencing life and being a human emotional being? If we get caught in the struggle of wanting to know why you are here, what is my purpose; it can stop or slow down in the creative process and keep us limited.

The Great American Classic "The Wizard of Oz" is a story that has lived on generation after generation, portraying simple but treasured values. The story includes our innocence, our search for identities, stimulates the imagination with dreams, faith and hope of possibilities. There was magic from this movie that touched and filled the hearts of many and still does to this day. In this film they also showed us that fear and darkness can be overcome by following our hearts and trusting in the Divine.

Dorothy always had the power to go back to Kansas but she couldn't be told this because she wouldn't have believed it and had to learn this for herself. When she was asked what she had learned from this experience, her reply was "If I ever go looking for my heart any farther than my own backyard and it's not there, I really never lost it to begin with". Scarecrow's remark was "That's too easy".

The main theme of the movie was Dorothy, Tinman, Lion and Scarecrow were all looking for something outside of themselves. They then became aware; everything they were looking for was right within themselves and they didn't realize it until they experienced it. Another valuable realization was, making that divine connection through the heart space; home is where the heart is.

It does take courage to experience life on planet Earth, otherwise you wouldn't be here. We are all becoming aware of our divine birthrights and how to live from a space of truth. We are discovering new ways to create, which are much more powerful and life giving to ourselves and humanity as a whole. What experiences will you create in your story that can make a difference for your family, community, the evolution of man and most importantly for yourself?

The simplest truth; we have experiences, attach emotions to those experiences and this creates our story.

"We are not our story, we think we are and this brings us all kinds of sorrow, suffering and pain." (Peaceful Warrior, Dan Millman")

SNOWBALL
EFFECT

To further understand how our story was created, we need to take a deeper look within ourselves at how we perceive things. Perception is based on our interpretation of experiences and emotional attachment to those experiences. Have you ever perceived something different than someone else or didn't understand another person's perception?

Is our perception right, wrong, good or bad? Our perception is just that, a perception. Why is it important to become aware of our perceptions? Perceptions can turn into opinions that can snowball into deep beliefs that affect our lives and choices in many different areas and ways. Let's take a look at an example of a perception, snowball and its results.

> Let's take an example of a child that grows up in a family that was always fighting over money, with verbal, physical and emotional abuse. Mom and Dad end up getting a divorce,

mom is left with no child support and the responsibility of raising her children by herself. Mom was able to provide for the children, but experienced feelings of scarcity, worry, fear and lack surrounding the money, which is passed onto the children. (story)

Now let's take a look at combining all the experiences, emotions and perceptions surrounding money from this child's experience. Perceptions could be that money is bad, creates fighting, hurts people, it's scarce, fearful, causes worrying, suffering, abuse and other emotional experiences found in the emotional maze. This experience has now snowballed from simple perceptions and opinions into deep seated beliefs which became buried in the subconscious. If not healed, these beliefs or perceptions surrounding money could affect their life choices, experiences or relationships well into adulthood that they may not even be consciously aware of.

There are numerous beliefs surrounding money that are untrue because of negative experiences and perceptions. Money is evil or bad, only intelligent people have money, it's not possible to have money and be spiritual, feelings of not being good enough to have money and the list goes on and on. Can you see how the experiences started with perceptions, opinions and snowballed into stuck beliefs about money? Like everything else, money is energy, it doesn't do anything to anyone, and it's only a means of exchange. Blaming money will not change what you're currently experiencing.

Have you ever thought about your beliefs? Where they come from? How they affect your life? Are your beliefs true? Where your beliefs are stored? Why beliefs are so strong and powerful? If you have beliefs that are keeping you stuck and trapped? You may be pleasantly surprised to find out that the large majority of your beliefs don't even belong to you. They have been passed on from generation to generation, person to person, socially and globally. Remember, it's all about energy, energy moves whether it's in thoughts, beliefs or experiences.

The majority of our beliefs came from childhood and gathered momentum over the years. Some beliefs are also passed on from past lives, ancestors, media, friends, family and many other sources. Are any of our beliefs even real? Do beliefs change over the years? Can beliefs keep us trapped and stuck in repetitive patterns that no longer serve us? Can existing beliefs limit us from experiencing more rewarding experiences?

We also have beliefs that make us feel powerful, strong and give us hope, courage and strength. I'm quite sure that the majority of us would like to experience more empowering beliefs with ease and grace.

Whatever you believe will be attracted to you time and time again, whether that is good, bad, positive or negative. If you are experiencing lack, subconsciously or consciously, you send out that vibration in your thoughts, words, and expressions. That's what will return to you via people, experiences, places or things. Your energy frequencies are much like radio signals, if we want to experience something different, it's necessary to change the station.

There are perceptions, opinions and beliefs that surround absolutely everything you see, feel, hear or touch. A key to working with your beliefs, once again is to realize you aren't your perceptions, beliefs, experiences or story. This awareness will help make it easier to release or change the beliefs that aren't true and don't serve you in a positive way.

I have found many, many beliefs stuck in the subconscious that people were not even aware of on a conscious level. Here's a few examples of stuck beliefs affecting people's lives; wanting healthy, happy, joyful relationships, yet are holding onto hidden beliefs that keep attracting them into experiences of abusive and controlling relationships.

Beliefs that were causing self-sabotaging, self-destruction, unforgiveness, and self-hatred connected to stuck, traumatic experiences.

There are many that have experienced being a nun or priest in a past lifetime and there are stuck vows, beliefs and oaths that are affecting them in this lifetime.

Beliefs such as I don't need anyone, I can do everything myself.

Stored beliefs that women can't be successful, it's not allowed.

These are just small samples, there are many, many stored beliefs consistently playing in the background.

Then, there are those that have beliefs that empower them. Do you know anyone that seems to have everything flowing to them easily, effortlessly and they seem to have it all? Maybe that person is always in the right place, at the right time. Still there are others that seem to turn everything they touch into gold.

Maybe you know a person that always seems to be happy, upbeat and enjoying life. Then there are those that don't even seem like they need to try, everything flows for them. These people have some very powerful beliefs that are helping them create their life experiences. Where did they get them? Why don't we all have them? Chances are they were raised from childhood with these beliefs or they made choices to change beliefs that were causing suffering.

One of the easiest ways to become aware of which beliefs are empowering and which are disempowering you is to take some time looking at your existing life.

Are there problems with relationships or family? You might ask yourself, how you feel about money. Are you working a job you like? Are you happy, having fun and allowing playtime? Do you feel like something is missing in your life or holding you back? Do you have friends you love to share with?

If you are not experiencing life as you would like to, then there is a large possibility there are some stuck or hidden beliefs that are affecting the quality of your life experiences. **News flash**, beliefs don't need to make sense. Beliefs don't just go away! People are willing to die or kill others because of their beliefs!

Beginning to question our beliefs can bring them into conscious awareness and then we can decide which ones are serving us and which ones need our attention.

The power of attention and intention will help you to become more aware of your current beliefs.

All the positive affirmations in the world won't change a belief or an experience. If we believe something isn't possible, it's not. Isn't it interesting how the placebo effect works so well? If we believe in miracles, we will see them and experience them, if we don't, they will go unnoticed, even if they have occurred.

So the real core of change lies in finding our core beliefs, our own truth, becoming congruent consciously and subconsciously with what we would like to experience and begin creating the preferred reality, mentally, emotionally and physically.

Where are beliefs stored? We have a conscious mind and a subconscious mind. The subconscious mind is like the computer data bank. Just like a computer, there is no right, wrong, good or bad in the data bank.

All experiences, beliefs and your life story are located in the subconscious whether you are aware or not. The subconscious never sleeps, it just keeps recording everything you experience twenty four/seven. There are several different tools and methods that can help you access your data bank to find out what beliefs may be affecting you in a negative way. Research results have proven time and time again that changing a belief from a conscious level can be limiting, difficult and those changes tend not to last.

Anytime you have a thought in your mind, it automatically goes to the subconscious looking for data related to that thought and sends out the energy signal. Remember there is no right, wrong, good or bad in the data bank. For instance, if you feel overweight and constantly reiterate that in you conscious mind, that message will keep going to the data bank looking for ways to satisfy your request to be overweight, whether that be with overeating, cravings or numerous other ways.

A great example of how the subconscious mind is influenced: when you say the word diet (first three letters, die), that sends a message to your subconscious to protect you by holding onto the weight you currently are experiencing. What happens when you say, I need to lose weight? Even if we lose the weight, we have to find it again because it's lost. See how the subconscious wants to protect us and how it interprets everything so literal.

Let's look at another example, say you go to work, with an attitude that no matter what you do it's not good enough. You may not be aware of it consciously but the energetic signals (thoughts, beliefs, words, actions) are transmitting that you are not good enough. That energy then attracts people, events and experiences to prove you are not good enough. Maybe your boss criticizes you more than usual, maybe a co-worker criticizes your work, a customer criticizes your knowledge on a product or you are told you don't qualify for a promotion.

Let's look at another example. I will never meet the person of my dreams or experience a good relationship. Those thoughts go to the data bank and guess what; you get exactly what you asked for, dysfunctional relationships.

These are a few examples of perceptions that turned into beliefs that got buried, stuck or trapped in the data bank. These old beliefs will keep playing over and over, like a broken record, creating experiences that match those energy frequencies being sent out, until we change our beliefs connected to what we are trying to create.

Create it in the mind and thus you make it real. The subconscious doesn't know what isn't real, it's a data bank. There are several scientific studies and data to support this theory. There are studies where basketball players used their imagination to practice making baskets only in their mind and they did just as well as those that actually practiced on the court.

There are several other similar scientific experiments and studies available to further understand quantum energy.

One of the problems with our perception is that it's very limited and biased. It depends on what we have experienced or what we see, hear, touch and feel. Another problem, a lot of perceptions and beliefs are just untrue.

For example, just because a person is dressed in a suit, this makes them more powerful, intelligent and successful (perception).

The moon controlling and influencing the tides in the ocean is another example of unseen energy. We don't see the moon's energy and have limited knowledge on how it affects us but we know it does. We are limited by the eyes and senses that just see a large body of water; we call the ocean (perception).

Another example might be, just because someone has gone to college and has a degree; they are more intelligent than others. Perceptions create beliefs in some that, if I don't go to college, I will never amount to anything and will never be intelligent.

There are millions of dollars spent on marketing to find ways to influence our perceptions and beliefs, all the way from the laundry soap we use, clothes we wear, how we live, what we have, our relationships, political views and the list goes on and on.

Have you noticed that there are more commercials, marketing, advertising than there has ever been? All empty spaces whether that be on the media, internet, television or anywhere else are being filled with buy this or buy that. At any given time your subconscious is being filled with all this data.

Many say they are unaffected, not true. Have you noticed even at the movies that before the movie even begins the energy that is being portrayed is buy this or buy that? One of the biggest problems with all this marketing at the movies, all your senses are being activated.

Remember, the more senses included in an experience, the more powerful it is. This is also part of the reason subliminal messages at the movies use to be so powerful. Have you noticed how this is affecting you or your children, it may be subtle? Another thing about the movies that makes this energy so powerful is that there is no mute button and your attention is more focused.

Checking your email? How many messages do you have flashing, stationary or being displayed at any given time? Now, they are even moving advertisements across the screen and layering them. This is all energy being portrayed in one way or another.

So you might say, so what? We are overloaded and overwhelmed with way too much information and influenced so much by all the marketing techniques. Is it any wonder with this constant stimulation that it's hard to get back in touch with our heart and make choices from it rather that all the outside influences? Can you see why it's necessary to go within to find your beliefs and your truth in all areas of your life? All these outside influences can keep us on a constant search of everything outside ourselves, wondering what is true for me.

What if you are the ideal weight?

What if you are a woman that feels sexy in long johns?

What if the old refrigerator works fine?

What if your relationship is just fine?

What if you love peaceful quiet time?

A good movie that comes to mind is the "Runaway Bride" where she is so busy doing what everyone expects her to do that she doesn't even know what kind of eggs she likes. How about the mom that has been doing so much for her employer, family and relationships that she lost track of her own dreams and herself?

Please don't think that it's not good to have perceptions, opinions and beliefs, it's part of the human experience. It's important to be careful not to buy into beliefs that don't serve you and end up snowballing into negative experiences time and time again.

Awareness, awareness and more awareness of your perceptions and beliefs will lead you back to your own heart and reunite you with the infinite being you are!

"The power of beliefs can destroy, control, entrap or empower."

WORDS

What is the recipe of your life? Would you agree that it's composed of experiences, emotions and stories? What are some of the ingredients for experiencing life? Would you agree that intentions, perceptions, beliefs, feelings, thoughts and choices ultimately give you the power to create your own reality? Sometimes the answers are so simple we overlook their power. Now, let's take a deeper look into what else influences our lives on a deeper level.

Words influence and affect us on very deep levels but few recognize the power words have in the world of energy. Words are energy, part of human experience and the creation process. Words just seem to flow while we are having conversations or expressing ourselves. Why is this a big deal?

How you express or don't express yourself in words is a clue to understanding where you are in life, how you are feeling about yourself and others.

Have you ever noticed your own vocabulary? To make long lasting, successful changes in life, it's necessary to notice the energy of words, your own vocabulary, how you are affected by words and other people's words.

Words affect us because of our perceptions and beliefs which are directly connected to our own experiences. Change your mind, beliefs or perceptions and you will experience something totally different. Easier than it sounds, right?

An important thing to understand is that words don't always have the same meaning to everyone and that's ok! The word "Love" has many different meanings, is portrayed in a variety of different ways and depends on your experiences connected to it. For instance, if you were raised in a family that love was never expressed, your feelings about the word "Love" will be very different from someone who was raised in a family where love was expressed freely, in many different ways.

It's not the words themselves that affect us. What is meant by this? If we didn't have any meaning for a word, no experiences connected to the word, we wouldn't even be affected. How about a word that you don't know what it means? It doesn't affect you, right? So you see it's the attachments, meanings we give words and our experiences that give these words power.

Let's say in your family there were words that we associate with love shared freely, like "I Love you" and there were gestures of love that were shown frequently, like a special meal just for you, flowers, holding hands, a kiss, kind words, hugs, a special card or a gift, just because. Now your association with the word love and the energy of love shown in the example above can help you to understand some of the ways you can express love from within to the outward expression. Now let's say that you know someone who has never experienced these things, will the word love mean the same thing?

In the example above it's important to note that the expression of love (energy) came from within, in many different forms and was expressed outward. If you are relying on words or gifts to make you feel loved, it will only be short lived and lose its value within a short time.

The truth is the word love as we experience it is quite different than "I AM LOVE". This love has no words, definitions and is not limited by our experiences or attached to people, places and things.

There are words that can make us feel powerful, sad, happy, strong, weak, fearful and many more emotions from our emotional maze. The dominant words we use continually to describe our lives and share our stories are those affecting us the most.

There is nothing new here that you don't already know but it's necessary to review our awareness of the words that we are using to empower or disempower ourselves.

Words (energy) sent out into the universe come back with the same words in the form of experiences. We can communicate words but until each person experiences those words energetically in an experience, they won't have a perception of that energy.

How do you know what chocolate tastes like if you have never experienced it? How will you ever know what anger feels like until you have experienced it? How will you know what leather feels like until you have felt it? How will you know what riding a horse feels like until you have experienced it? All things you need to experience for yourself.

Now that we understand that words are energy that have power and the energy of words is attracted back to us, we can now understand how they get trapped energetically in our being.

How about the words trapped from a family feud that have been stuck there for years? How about those hurtful words dad or mom said or didn't say that never went away? You know if you have stuck energy (words), they just keep resurfacing time and time again, pushing your buttons, re-enacting the same old experiences and memories.

When we look at the bright side of stuck, buried energy, we understand and know which words are affecting our lives and pushing our buttons; we can then heal and release them.

Experiences and words affecting you that got stuck in the subconscious, which you are not aware of consciously can be accessed and healed. Sometimes people think they have let the words and experiences go but will find by working with the subconscious programing, some of those old words and experiences just got buried and are still affecting them.

A common example of this is someone being told they were stupid in their younger years.

That simple statement (words), especially from a loved one can stick like glue following them the rest of their life. They may not realize it consciously, but it's a hidden energetic experience affecting them and their life. It may show up as not being able to experience certain things because you aren't smart enough, not being able to have their own business, not smart enough to go to college, feeling something is wrong with them, fear of humiliation, fear of speaking up and the list goes on and on.

Usually when the core experience is released and healed there is a domino effect in all areas of your life. The best part of healing something like the example above, your consciousness expands and opens up a whole new paradigm of possibilities. As long as you remain trapped in the words and experiences, that energy keeps going out to the universe and returns with more of the same of that which you want to be freed from.

It's kind of like the more you chase money, the further it eludes you or the harder you try, the worse things get and this leads to dead end cycles that keep us trapped and stuck, even though we want to move on. The tiger chasing his tail or going around and around in the same circle until an aha moment arises.

It might help you to learn that the vast majority of stuck energy, words and experiences are trapped from birth to six or seven years old. Finding and healing those experiences and words in childhood memories which got stuck and trapped can be an unbelievable, freeing experience. Then, you will be free to experience wonderful opportunities that were blocked because of some simple words that got stuck. Can simple words have a profound effect on us, YES!

Doing the work is not always simple but can be. One simple clearing can make a tremendous difference in your life, experiences and story.

What if you were taught the only way you can experience life is through struggle and that limiting belief, word and experience (energy) was healed in your subconscious? What if your life and experiences could flow with ease and grace without holding on for dear life of that which no longer serves you?

Our world is filled with titles, the energy of labels and words that can control, limit our lives, keep us stuck and trapped, unable to expand our consciousness to more empowering, rewarding experiences and expressions. We can spend a whole lifetime resisting and reacting instead of creating.

One of the funny things about our reacting and resistance connected to words is that the majority of the time, those words, labels and titles don't even belong to us. Take a moment to think about the last time you reacted to something someone said and ask yourself, was that your stuff or were they just acting out their stuff?

Sometimes there will be experiences attracted to us as a test, to see if we have really learned the lesson that was hidden under all the drama. This can be just like experiencing a movie, understanding the main theme that is being portrayed.

An example of that might be, if we have been working on the word guilt, some direct experience or experiences will show up to see if guilt is still present. Another example might be working on the word blame. Experiences and opportunities to blame yourself or others will present themselves to see how we react or respond. If your buttons were pushed by the experiences, more healing work is necessary to see where you may be still emotionally attached to an old experience.

Blame is one of those destructive words from the emotional maze that helps no one! We blame the government, blame our parents, blame ourselves, blame others blame our family, blame our friends and this emotional expression is like mud that keeps us stuck.

Blaming others just keeps us going around and around solving nothing, creating nothing. One time or another in our lives, everyone has experienced being blamed for something they didn't do and that experience was supposed to teach us a valuable lesson. Did we learn or are we still blaming? Could there be an experience that got stuck in which we were blamed for something we didn't do in our younger years that has never been released or healed? Blame is a huge destructive word in the emotional maze and usually ends up including an even more destructive word "fear".

Remember whatever we feed grows. If we continually share words like "I am broke" that becomes our reality. If we continually use words describing suffering, we get to experience more suffering. If we continually share words of judgment, we get to be judged. Constantly sharing words of criticism, we get to experience criticism.

Is it really this simple? Why not take a few days to listen to your inner dialog and the words you are using in conversations and see what comes up? Understanding and awareness of how important words can be is something simple each person can do for themselves to find their own truth. If we use every opportunity to use empowering words in our own life for ourselves and others, we will raise the energy of the world and make our own experiences much more powerful and rewarding.

"Words are only words, it's what you do with them that matters."

EMPATHY

So far we have covered that life is filled with different experiences (jelly beans) that are stacked on top of each other like building blocks, we are emotional beings with a choice of many different emotions we can access at any given time from our treasure box and this is how we create our story.

We have also covered how our power lies within the awareness of our perceptions, intentions, beliefs, choices, words, thoughts and it's our responsibility to become the creators we were meant to be.

We learned how the snowball affect can influence and control our lives. We also learned that we aren't our emotions, experiences, the many different roles we play, titles or tags and how stuck trapped energy snowballs into all areas of our lives, attracting back to us whatever energy vibrations are being sent out (positive or negative).

Now let's take a look at how the energy of a simple word "empathy", can have such a profound influence and affect in our lives in so many different ways.

A definition of empathy; "Empathy is the capacity to recognize feelings that are being experienced by another being".

Now let's take a look at the difference between experiencing empathy and an empathetic person. It can be difficult to differentiate what belongs to an empathetic person and what doesn't. This is because empathetic people are particularly sensitive to others' needs, emotions and pain. Empathetic people are extremely tuned into the emotions of those surrounding them. They may not even be aware that they possess this skill. They have the ability to feel others' emotions and internalize them within their own being and make them their own.

The loss of their own identity becomes a very draining experience as they become more and more sensitive to others' needs. An empathetic person will find that they live in their emotions and emotional body the majority of time.

Have you ever felt sad and didn't have anything in particular that you personally experienced that could have created this? Have you ever had a conversation with someone and days, weeks, years later you are still experiencing the feelings and mind chatter?

Have you ever watched a movie and later you were still feeling anxiety or other emotions connected to the movie? Have you ever felt someone's pain in your body or holding onto pain that doesn't belong to you? Have you ever listened to someone's experience of sickness and experienced it yourself? Have you ever felt someone's suffering so much that you felt you had to fix it? Do you wake up always thinking of others, become consumed with thoughts of others throughout your day and go to sleep with the same scenario on a consistent basis?

It's one thing to experience empathy and release it but it's a totally different experience to be an empathetic person and hold onto someone's energy in your being. We are energy beings and energy moves in, out and around us mentally, physically and emotionally on a consistent basis with or without our awareness.

Awareness is your key to understanding which energy is yours and which energy belongs to someone else and their journey. If you claim any energy in your being and hold onto that energy, you get to experience it, maybe not consciously but it will be hidden in the subconscious, affecting your life.

Having empathy is a good thing and life without it would be a pretty heartless experience but claiming other people's energy can lead to exhaustion, being lost, confusion, sickness and numerous other negative experiences. This can happen very easily and even without your conscious awareness of it. It slips in here and there without you even realizing that it's happening. This empathy starts out as an innocent emotion and before you know it, becomes a way of life. Becoming an empathetic person can be a great blessing if you understand what is happening and learn to release any empathetic energy that doesn't belong to you.

Several people that I have done energy clearings for have found themselves to be empathetics. There was a lady that I worked with who had been in a great deal of pain for several years. She had tried many different alternatives and was very limited in her daily life and business. We discovered, while doing energy clearings, she was empathetically experiencing in her body, pain because of ongoing telephone conversations with her mom. The telephone conversations consisted of ongoing experiences for years of sickness connected with her mom and a sick aunt.

After we did the clearings for this empathetic experience, all the pain she had been enduring for a very long time went away, it wasn't hers. She now pays close attention to which experiences belong to her and which ones don't.

While energy clearing another lady, we discovered her depression wasn't even hers, it was empathically being experienced from her lineage. She is no longer experiencing depression. These are just a couple of examples. I have cleared many empathetic people that became stuck and trapped in experiences and emotions that didn't belong to them.

Many people that have been raised in child abuse or that have experienced abusive relationships are also very empathetic. It became a way of life used to protect themselves. Learning to be able to experience someone's emotions empathically, became a developed, practiced skill for some, to say the right things and do the right things in order to avoid the anger, rage or physical abuse. They were just trying to stay out of harm's way. Even after leaving experiences like this, those emotions, hurt, pain, suffering and trauma can still be buried deep inside. If this energy is still trapped and stuck, it can affect you in many different areas for an entire lifetime.

As part of my journey through the school of life, I too became an empathetic person that was raised in child abuse and it took over my life, hidden in the back ground.
I wasn't at all conscious that I had taken on this role, just thought I was being thoughtful and wanted to help others by being kind and thinking of them.

Maybe the road signs were there throughout an amazing amount of pain and suffering but I was clueless. Because of many years of collecting empathetic energy of others, it has taken many hours and years of inner work, clearings and forgiveness to help me release what was not mine, to find my own identity and path.

First and foremost it took me many years to understand and realize that I chose to experience child abuse, being a sensitive person, being an empathic person, people pleaser and I have taken responsibility for all those choices and more. This deep inner work takes courage, awareness, authenticity, time, patience and consistency to experience freedom to be yourself. It's not something that can be done one time and you're finished, it's an ongoing process of choosing a new way of life, freedom to be you.

Like many, I was raised in a dysfunctional family which included child abuse mentally, physically, verbally and emotionally. Rage, anger and physical abuse was the common theme at our house and living in a state of fear was a way of life. There were no specific triggers; it could be anything and everything that would ignite the rage and the experiences that followed.

My mom's side of the family was peaceful and large parts of dad's family were mean, abusive, angry controlling people. This isn't to say there wasn't dysfunction in my mom's side of the family, even though they were peaceful, but there was no rage and physical abuse that I am aware of.

I don't need to explain child abuse or any other kind of abuse to those that have experienced it, you already know all too well the hurt, pain, suffering, devastation and trauma connected to such an experience. The reason I have included my experience is to help others understand where people pleasing and being an empathetic person can start and where it can lead.

In order to release and energetically heal the many different facets of this experience, as in any negative experience, it's necessary to find the beginning, core or seeds that were planted. The core could be in the womb, at a very young age, past life experiences, carried through lineage or ancestry. Healing the last abuse or experience will only be a bandage for a very deep wound.

An example of an extreme case of an empathetic experience that was brought to my attention, was a child that went blind at two years of age, after there had been physical abuse involving her parents. She no longer wanted to see. It was just too traumatic for her sensitive soul. She is now working at regaining her eyesight.

I really don't know which came first, the people pleasing or being an empathetic person. It really doesn't matter, they were both experiences I chose for reasons that are way beyond my comprehension. Maybe it was to evolve, maybe in another lifetime I was the abuser or maybe it was a contract made before I decided to visit planet earth.

Both the people pleasing and being an empathic person, slowly and steadily grew over the years. Without realizing it consciously, this became a way of life year after year until some pretty devastating, traumatic experiences (gifts) forced me to go on an inward journey, within myself to understand what was going on at a deeper level.

Many people that are giving, caring people, healers or caregivers are experiencing being empathics. They hold onto other people's stories, experiences and energy inside their being and don't realize on a conscious level that this is even happening, making them sick, creating stress or disharmony. Like I said earlier, it becomes a way of life and begins to stack like blocks, layer on top of layer for many years. Many empathetic people believe they are doing good things for others and that makes them feel good inside.

Please don't misunderstand that I am saying there is something wrong with helping others, we are here to experience, learn, evolve, grow and serve. It does feel good to help others in need, there is nothing like it! There is a difference between helping others and the empathetic, people pleasing experiences. An important thing to remember, if you lose you and leave yourself out of the equation, don't serve your own needs first, eventually, you could experience feeling drained, confused, lost and emotionally out of balance.

I could go on and on with story after story of many individuals that have experienced or are experiencing being connected to the role of an empathetic person.

What a disempowering experience, to choose this way of life, with all the sorrow, hurt, pain and suffering that follows. Maybe you already know you are an empathetic person, have experienced this and didn't realize or understand what was happening.

It's my intention to bring awareness and understanding to those that have claimed such a disempowering experience without consciously knowing they have done so. Remember, this is energy, experiences and emotions hidden in the subconscious and it doesn't belong to you. I would like to encourage those that are empathetically experiencing life to move forward, make a new choice and claim their own life, light and ability to create. This will not only help themselves but their families, the children, loved ones but also the world. How can we empower ourselves and others when we are stuck with empathetic emotional energy controlling our lives?

I wish it was as easy as just consciously saying "NO MORE". I have found after many years of experiences and energy work with others, it takes courage, strength, patience, ongoing work and a great love of yourself to set yourself free to experience a much more rewarding, happier, healthier and abundant life. Oh by the way, I do say the words "NO MORE" now and then to remind myself when I get off track and as I learn to release that which doesn't belong to me.

"Access Consciousness" Has a little saying "Who does this belong to?" for three consecutive days you ask yourself that question for every thought you have. After three days you will be more than surprised, the majority of those thoughts were not even yours. It's a very simple tool but powerful. Another tool I have found to be powerful is asking "Is this my business, God's (source or whatever you call your higher power) business or your business?"

Sometimes when we think we are helping others and mean well, we are actually doing more harm to ourselves and them. Each person has divine support, trillions of cells with divine knowledge, their own guidance available and their own journey. How could we possibly know what is in their best interest or what their journey includes? Is it possible, no matter how much we love someone to change them, think for them, make choices for them or fix their life? We can love them, honor their journey, support them, send them prayers, but in the end, their journey is theirs.

Let's now take a look at how all our experiences, emotions, words and stories influence our health, mentally, physically, spiritually and emotionally. Remember, we are talking about energy; everything is energy that travels at different speeds, frequencies, patterns and vibrations.

"Your greatest internal satisfaction will come from creating your own journey".

HEALTH

Health is such a small word which as an enormous, profound affect and power across the globe. The topic of health is like a huge tree with unlimited roots and branches that are inter-connected to the earth, divine consciousness and everything in-between.

There is an overwhelming amount of information, marketing, different beliefs, options, perceptions and experiences that vary from person to person across the globe.

The constant flow of information of what foods to eat, what foods not to eat, the latest fad, medicines, nutrients, what is good for us and what is not.

Exercise, meditate, drink lots of water, diet, salt, no salt, organic, non-organic, gmo's, gluten, this oil is good for you, this oil is bad, aspartame, high fructose corn syrup, msg, soy is good for you, now soy isn't good for you and as you very well know, the list goes on and on, like a bottomless pit of should and shouldn't.

Is it any wonder there is so much confusion of what to do and what not to do in order to be able to live in a healthy state, while being bombarded on a consistent basis with information regarding health, whether it be right, wrong, good or bad?

I have spent many years researching, studying and applying different alternative healing resources, healing tools, techniques and modalities for improving my own life and the lives of others. My main focus and intention was to find ways to improve the quality of life with grace, quickly, easily and share healing tools that others can use themselves. Alternative healing in whatever form that may be, tools or methods that really work on a deep level for long term healing and the search continues to this day, always learning, applying, being open to improvement and expansion.

This journey has lead me down many different paths, looking for truth and answers that would help those who wanted to take responsibility for their health, life, find their truth and be a part of their own wellness journey. This research is an ongoing process that has no limitations.

I found energy healing is a vital part of the healing process, regardless of the other forms of healing being used. This includes nutrients, herbs, homeopathic and the many other forms of alternatives available.

Many people are becoming actively involved in making changes in their own lives and health that will not only benefit themselves, their families and others but will ultimately change the world in one way or another.

It is my belief, as we all gain more understanding, awareness connected to the flow of energy; expand our consciousness to all the possibilities, our state of health will improve dramatically.

The newest and latest health conscious movement includes energy healing in several different forms, with each individual being an integral part of that process. Learning about yourself, finding your own answers from within, and connecting to source energy is critical. Energy healing is nothing new, in fact it's ancient and it was stated in the bible that we could heal ourselves. Now our awareness, beliefs and perceptions are expanding to include this energy health conscious movement.

As a society, we have gotten use to tagging absolutely everything. As we tag everything, attach drama, symptoms and continue to feed it in conversations, give it power, we are actually feeding that energy and it grows. This applies to anything and everything, as mentioned earlier; it is the universal law of attraction at work.

 Have you ever wondered why everyone gets the "flu" at the same time around the world? Why some people never get the "flu"? Where "flu" season came from? Could there be any correlation to hearing it's "flu" season, it's time for your "flu" shots or big signs and banners that say get your "flu" shots here. Remember, the subconscious has no since of humor and takes all those signs, tags and conversations literally. Could there be many things tagged as the "flu" because we don't know what else to call them?

Programing works very well and hides out beneath the conscious level, affecting our lives on a consistent basis without us even knowing, little by little, day by day, year after year. What if we decided there was no such thing as "flu" season and discontinued feeding that energy? Maybe, we should have a wellness season. Reminder; words and thoughts are energy.

There are several energy healing sources that work with expanding the consciousness beyond our limited perceptions. I encourage people to start asking the question "Is this really true or is this really mine?" As a whole, we all need to stop feeding and giving energy to things that control and disempower us.

Stress is another great example of a tag that has gained a lot of power over the years. Now the word "stress" is used for anything and everything. What do you think is causing all this stress? Law of attraction at work, send out the signal of stress and what returns? The answer is black and white; your wish is my command, things to stress over or about. Again, a simple word that is all about choices we make. The word stress has become a mainstream conversation piece and an excuse for anything and everything. The real source of stress then remains hidden, creating more stress.

Ok, so now what? When we have gone beyond the experience of tagging and naming, we can begin to see things with new eyes, awareness and understanding. Energy work is all about becoming familiar, having a sense of knowing and tuning in on the energy that is present at any given time. It's like tuning into the channel on the radio. It's easier than you think.

If you close your eyes and do an internal scan of your body, what do you sense? Is the energy light or heavy? Is there energy that is dense? Is there anxiety? Is there energy that is dark, feels stuck or trapped? Is there energy that feels blocked, tight or tense? Could there be cramped, rigid, confused energy that has become trapped in the body or mind? How about stiffness, pain, swelling, inflammation or nervous energy?

Please don't worry about doing it wrong, you are really the only one that knows what is happening inside your body, mind or energy field. You have the power to do this! You might have to practice this for a while but soon you will become very familiar of the unseen energy and how it's affecting you. Those that have turned off their feelings, need to start with small steps, sometimes those small steps can make huge changes.

Maybe you are aware in other areas and have never noticed your own energy field.

How about the horse you could feel something was wrong with it? How about that engine that doesn't sound right? How about that funny feeling that there is something wrong with the food you are eating? Maybe, it's the guests that are coming to visit or something that just doesn't feel right in your house.

We all have the skills and abilities to tune in, but a lot of the time, it is turned off and we are on automatic pilot, distracted by this or that, somewhere else and not in the present. Energy work does require that we start becoming aware of that unseen energy in and around us. Usually, there are many energy signs before sickness or disease sets in, but we don't pay attention until that energy creates symptoms that demand our attention. Even then, we still have a choice of how to go about the healing process.

Do we mask energy problems with excuses, other sources or empower ourselves by finding the seed that created the problem in the first place? Are we ready to take a look at what we learned from the experience, release it and move on?

Let's take an example of going to the produce section of the grocery store. Did you know that if you are paying attention while in the produce section of the store, without distractions, your body, mind and senses will be drawn to whatever color or food you need?

If you're attracted to the lemons and the color yellow, that is your natural ability and a signal telling you what you need. Needing yellow could signify the need to do some internal cleansing. Go with your first impressions; try not to second guess your intuition. Are you attracted to that big red apple or the red tomatoes? Are you attracted to the greens or the oranges?

Your senses also know if the energy of that produce is good; such as that big tomato or the watermelon that has no flavor. Many foods with no flavor have been messed with and feel kind of empty when you hold them. You can also start asking your higher self if this product is good but I have found that you need to be pretty specific in what you are asking. Maybe it's a good product but not good for you. My point here is that you can't trick the body, senses or natural sense of knowing.

It's always fascinating to watch people in the smelly isles at the stores, looking for candles, room deodorizes or other scented items. They may be coughing, sneezing and when talking, it sounds like their nose is plugged from the senses reacting to the smells. Maybe there are children in the shopping cart experiencing the same thing. The senses are reacting to the energy in that area and if the senses are continually exposed to these artificial smells, there is a large possibility of ongoing sinus problems, breathing problems and numerous other complications. Your senses react with different symptoms, letting you know something is wrong with that energy.

Now how about the relationship you may be experiencing that is draining you or the relationship that makes you feel good, happy, alive and full of life the majority of the time? Are you in a relationship of constantly experiencing fighting or do you share conversations? Are you being controlled by others, significant others or are you trying to control others and their lives? You might ask what all this has to do with health. Anything and everything that has to do with energy affects our health in one way or another. Whether that be our lifestyles, food we eat, job experiences or relationships. The energy of the thoughts and experiences goes into our body and energy field at many different levels, frequencies and vibrations. Some of this energy just dissipates, flows out into the cosmos and some of the energy gets trapped in the body. The more any negative energy is sent via thoughts, experiences or words into the body, the more likely it is that the energy will get stuck, which could possibly cause sickness or disease.

An example of this might be: if you

consistently tell yourself there is something wrong with you. That information goes to the subconscious (data bank with no emotions) and is perceived as something you are asking for. Your wish is my command, you might say, is a good metaphor for the subconscious mind. It may have never been your thoughts to begin with. If you consistently tell yourself you are angry, living in a state of anger, you may get to experience more of the same and that anger energy has a direct line to your liver or blood. What if that is something that has been passed on through the blood line and it could be energetically cleared and healed providing you with the opportunity for a new choice? An example might be my blood is boiling or the development of high blood pressure from suppressed and buried accumulated anger. If this energy is experienced continually, it could affect your health sooner or later.

There is plenty of data, research and information that is now available on how your beliefs, thoughts, experiences and words can make you sick or create disease.

What if the simplest way to becoming a healthier and happier you is by your understanding and awareness of energy? What if we have added way too much drama, not believed in ourselves, complicated our lives by constantly being side tracked with tags, conversations, stories, beliefs and marketing? What if the answers are so simple and we have made them complex by constantly struggling in the analytical mind that created the problem to start out with?

What if changing that job, releasing that sabotaging relationship, paying more attention to your breathing, staying in the now, paying attention to your thoughts, words and experiences was the answer we are all looking for to experience a healthier state of being.

YES, beliefs, experiences, emotions, words, being an empathetic and stories have a great amount of influence when it comes to our health.

YES, music, the news, mass consciousness, marketing, conversations, other outside sources also have influence when it comes to our health.

YES, relationships, programing, our ancestry, past lives, parents, and family relations can affect our health.

One of the keys to better quality of life and health is to start becoming aware of those energy frequencies that are affecting your life and wellbeing. It may sound complex but a few small changes can make a huge difference in our health. Remember, as long as we are stuck in the emotions, drama, stories, struggles and experiences that created the sickness, illness, disease in the first place, it's highly unlikely you can experience something else. Change your mind, change your life.

The rewards of becoming energy aware are

many. Over time you will find you are automatically attracted to whatever you need. The energy work will automatically lift your spirit; makes you feel lighter, stronger and healthier.

After raising your energy vibration, you will not be attracted to those experiences that disempower you, make you feel bad or drained. As you raise your energy frequencies, you will find that you are drawn to different people, experiences and foods. This also opens the doors of more opportunities, abundance in all areas of your life and automatically expands your energy.

If you believe something is bad for you, it will be. If you believe something will make you sick, it will. Remember, the subconscious has no good, bad, right, wrong or emotions. The belief system is tremendously powerful. The subconscious is just trying to protect you and giving you exactly what you are asking for. Your wish is my command. The only resources your subconscious has are those of the past and past experiences. The resources in the subconscious are very limited, biased and restricted. The best resources are from the Divine, Higher Self, God, Source or whatever you want to call the greater power.

The body knows how to heal itself but if we keep storing stuck energy, limiting beliefs, replaying the same old records, that energy sabotages the healing process and makes it harder for the body to heal itself.

Does your Divine Intelligence know how to heal a cut or wound, do you have to tell it what to do? Does your blood flow without you even having anything to do with the process? Does your intestinal tract know how to eliminate and your digestive system know what to do with food? Blocked, stuck, stored, buried, dense, stagnant energy can interfere with the body's natural healing process. Where does that stuck energy come from? Once again, a huge part of that stuck energy is stored beliefs, thoughts, emotions, words and experiences that are trapped energetically in the body.

I use to be in a state of awe when talking to my sister who had multiple sclerosis. For several years she was a quadriplegic and she could barely speak, her speech was communicated garble as the disease progressed and she would communicate with her eyes.

I was amazed that her bodily functions kept on going beyond all the things we are told and none of those organs failed, regardless of not being able to move, eat good foods and all the standard beliefs. She had no bed sores and kept herself out of the nursing home with the help of caregivers and when she decided she was done with the experience and wanted to pass on at home, she did just that.

Within a week after that decision, she passed quietly and peacefully at her home. I was always amazed at her strength and that she spent many hours by herself, not even able to move or make a call and ask for help. Her caregivers were only there during the daytime hours.

When she woke up, she always had a smile on her face and one time I asked her how did she do this day after day, year after year? She told me she went shopping in her mind. She loved her music playing by her bedside continually. Yes, she had her moments but the majority of the time she was up, regardless of her experience. Never underestimate the power of the mind. Create it in the mind and thus you make it real. She was a living example of that.

My mom also died from multiple sclerosis but her journey was completely different than my sisters. She was a phenomenal, strong and courageous woman. Her journey included the experience of this devastating disease and raising three children by herself with very little help or money. I only wish that the tools and opportunities available today would have been there for my sister and mom.

Louise L. Hay has a book called "You Can Heal Your Life" this book has sold millions of copies. It is the only book that I know of that covers specific problems, probable causes and new thought patterns. It covers some of the mental patterns behind disease, illnesses and sicknesses.

Last but not least, if you need help it's important to ask your Higher Source for help, direction and guidance. They know what will be best for each of us and will send whatever we need. Because of our free will, we have to ask for help before they can send it and the help will come in the best form for us. Your answers and prayers may not show up the way you expect. We also need to be open to receiving that information and sometimes the answers are so simple, we miss them. That person, book, healer, information or tools will appear but after asking for their help, we need to trust, have faith and get out of our own way.

"Health is a state of consciousness with mind, body, spirit and soul intertwined."

REALITY

iMaGination
IS MORE IMPORTANT THAN KNOWLEDGE

What story have you created with your stacked experiences and emotions? Are you trapped or stuck in the snowball effect, creating the same scenario over and over? Are you an empathetic person living in other people's lives and stories? Are your words, beliefs, senses, perceptions, thoughts, choices and intentions aligned with what you would like to create or experience? Is your conscious mind congruent with your subconscious mind? Are you empowering yourself and others? Are you trapped in your logical mind or emotional body with a disengaged heart?

By now I hope you understand that the reality you have chosen to experience was created by you and you have the power to create any reality that you would like to experience, regardless of what you are experiencing at the moment. You are a powerful being with unlimited and infinite potential! I'm sure you have heard the expression "It's not the destination that is important, it's the journey".

Often times we get trapped into believing everything is only real if we can see, touch, feel and hear it. We know that there are many things that just work, we don't understand, know how or why, we just know! Some examples of this might be the cell phone, electricity, rotation of the planets, miracles, formation of a baby in the womb or all the wonders of nature.

Is there anything that has ever been created into reality that didn't first start in the mind? The pictures and thoughts came, emotions were added, along with confidence, faith and a real strong belief it was possible. Maybe you can remember wanting that first car or bicycle, you thought about it, took some action, believed it was possible and it became reality.

We have all heard different people's success stories, how they overcame challenges and moved forward to create into reality whatever they wanted to experience.

Their stories empower us, make us feel good and touch a deep place within our hearts, reminding us of possibilities outside our limited perceptions and beliefs.

Many times the stories we hear will only inspire us for a short time. Why is that? Once again, we are creative beings and the only way we can experience is through our own emotions, dreams and journey. Yes, there are people, places and things that can help motivate, inspire and give us hope but ultimately it has to be our creation.

Can anyone create that bicycle, car, relationship, dream, business or anything else from their mind for you? Many times when others try to create what they think you want, that will be met with disappointment and will not give you that deep sense of "I did it"! There are a lot of healthy feelings, beliefs and emotions that go with those simple little words.

What is reality and what isn't can be elusive, controversial, create confusion, keep us stuck and trapped in a state of being, believing and perceiving, whatever we are experiencing at this time is all there is, it's our only choice and there is no way out.

This is often experienced because our fear of pain and suffering is greater than our belief that we can create and experience something new. There will be lots of excuses and justification for holding onto that which seems to have us trapped but the bottom line is the word, fear.

Can you experience anything new until you have released the old and created the new? Maybe it was getting fired from your job, maybe it was an affair, a friend betraying you, divorce, sickness, disease or losing your home before you could allow yourself to create something new. I think it would be fair to say that the majority of us would like to have the new come in and then we will let go of the old, sorry that's not the way it works.

Why is it that there are many that like taking the risks and failure is not even an option or included in their vocabulary? There are countless other examples of what we once thought to be true and real that have changed to a new reality, which is forever changing as we experience life? Isn't the global consciousness and the evolution of mankind evolving, changing into new realities, day by day, hour by hour, year by year?

Is it possible that reality only exists in our minds? Is it possible we are creating reality as we go? Is it possible we are limited in experiencing expansion of reality because of our senses, experiences and emotions? Can we experience any new reality until we have released the past, fear of the future and brought our awareness to the now? Do we need to get out of our own way, give up current stories in order to create new realities? Is it possible nothing is real???

Let's take a moment to look at another example of what is real and what is not.

Movies are a good example that can help us better understand how we are affected by what seems real, even though we know they are not. Movies have a way of igniting our senses; they use visuals, images, sounds, color, characters and stories. Without any of these components they would not have the same effect on us. Is there anyone who hasn't been affected by a movie at one time or another? Was the movie real? Could your body, mind or senses tell the difference between what was real and not real? Were you so much into the movie that you lost track of time and began experiencing the movie emotionally, without even being aware that it was affecting you? Did you want the good guy to win? Did the movie make you laugh? Did you get excited at the chase scene? Have you ever gone to a movie and became part of the portrayed experience so much in your heart that the tears of love or sadness became part of the experience? Have you ever felt joy or fear while experiencing a movie? Have you or someone you know, gone to a movie about sharks and ended up being scared to death of the ocean or sharks?

The movies seem real to our senses and mind but we know they aren't. Life is also a movie; we add the characters, sound, drama to our movies to give them life. Is our life reality or are we creating it as we go? Is the reality experienced yesterday the same today? If it's our creation, can we create the characters, story and dreams we would like to experience?

YES, YES, YES, Your dreams can become reality if you so choose. It's never too late no matter where you are now, your age or what your past experiences have been. Is your movie playing the old feud, past relationship stories, worry, fear, regret, guilt, slowing down what you truly wish to experience and is any of that who you are or is it even real?

"Reality is moving energy that is forever changing and can only be limited by the mind."

SELF
EMPOWERMENT

Let's take some time to review where our real power resides;

~ Consciousness, awareness and understanding that everything is energy, including thoughts and beliefs. Thoughts and beliefs have tremendous power, influencing our lives and wellbeing.

~ Some of the most powerful influences that affect us are; beliefs, perceptions, words, emotions, intentions, focused attention, feelings, thoughts and choices. These influences affect us whether we are aware of it or not.

~ Stacked experiences, stuck energy can snowball and keep us trapped, replaying the same old scenario that we want freedom from so badly, yet are unable to let go of.

~ Our current reality affects our life, health and future. Our reality becomes whatever we are focusing on, feeding, experiencing and creating, according to our beliefs which are stored in our data bank (subconscious).

~ Realizing that we aren't our story, relationships, the many different roles we play, our mind, our bodies, a title, our experiences, emotions or any attachments to outside influences of people, places or things can empower us and set us free to be the powerful spiritual creators we were meant to be.

In any given moment we have free will to change our story and detach from disempowering experiences. The law of attraction, "Your wish is my command" has no good, bad, right or wrong. Whatever energy is being telecasted will return in the form of experiences.

There is nothing wrong with us; we just get trapped in the energy of beliefs, thoughts, experiences which no longer serve us. The past keeps us stuck in emotions and the future thoughts usually create worry and fear.

Being in the now is our best choice and that takes energy awareness and practice. Eckharte Tolles' book "The Power Of Now" explains how learning to be in the now can empower us and change our lives.

Recognizing everything is energy, aligning with energy, which is forever flowing in frequencies, patterns, vibrations, waves and in many other forms, can help us in all areas of our lives. When we look through new eyes and expand our consciousness, it helps us not take everything to so personal.

Even though many have been taught and programed to struggle, work really hard, make everything complicated and as difficult as we possibly can, in order to succeed, this isn't true or necessary. Please don't misunderstand that we don't need challenges in life, we do. Simplicity is the key to flowing through those challenges with ease and grace. Kind of like a child's energy of innocence instead of rigid structured energy.

In this time of great change there are many people that are living in fear, feeling powerless or playing the role of victim. This is nothing to be ashamed of or embarrassed by, but it's important to understand that these states of mind just keep us disempowered, unable to experience the higher frequencies of love, joy or happiness.

If you are experiencing being trapped in these emotions, you aren't alone. The important thing is to bring those dark, heavy energy frequencies into the light so they can be healed and transformed. Observe, feel, and detach from these frequencies as quickly as you can rather than spiral downward playing in the darkness. It is guaranteed, playing in the darkness will only get darker and darker. Once anything is brought into awareness and light, it can no longer keep us trapped in its darkness.

Let's take a look at some of the areas that can be draining your energy, keeping you sidetracked, trapped and stuck, disempowering you, even if there is no conscious awareness.

Many claim that they are unaffected by the news, background music, dark movies, white noise, advertisements, social media, television and many other outside sources, but this isn't truth. Your own personal data bank (subconscious) and a little research and scientific studies will reveal quite the opposite.

We need quiet time to balance, restore and rejuvenate our energy beings. Often times when we don't take time for ourselves, regardless of the busy lifestyle or excuses, we will get to experience sickness, accidents or a host of other unpleasant experiences. "I'm too busy to take time for myself", have you ever used or heard those words?

When our energy is depleted and our tank is running half full or less, we not only disempower ourselves but also those around us. Can you ever really experience or know you, if you are in a constant state of stimulating energy frequencies of one sort or another.

Sometimes experiencing no stimulation connected to people, places and things, just being, can seem very lonely and uncomfortable. You alone with you, can feel fearful and scary. Many people retiring or retired are going through this experience and find it very uncomfortable. When you have been very busy or part of the system for a long time and you unplug, you can end up with a lot of unanswered questions. Maybe, "Is this all there is?", "What now?", "Who am I?" or in a state of feeling very disempowered.

One of the simplest, easiest, most empowering things you can do for yourself is to start becoming aware of what empowers you and what doesn't.

You might try asking your heart this simple question "Does this empower me or disempower me?" for anything and everything. Be careful not to come from the egoist mind state, this is power with grace and ease. Take time to get to know the true you, in your heart and start detaching from those draining energy fields, claim what empowers you and makes you truly feel good on the inside without outside attachments to people, places and things.

The ripple effect of each individual reclaiming their power will create strong families, communities, and empower others around the globe. Instead of having people trapped in fear, victimization, being controlled and feeling powerless, it will build a nation of creative individuals and possibilities. The power that is being portrayed here is that quiet, confident, radiate, strong, progressive energy for the good of all. We have to empower ourselves before we can ever help others empower themselves.

Another area we can empower ourselves is by recognizing our choices, becoming consciously aware and taking responsibility

for those choices on a consistent basis.
Many times, choices (free will) are made just
because, without really thinking, operating
on automatic pilot and being consistently
sidetracked in outside stimulation. Whether
we are willing to admit it or not, choices are
often times made because we want
approval, to fit in, to be included, for
attention or a multitude of other reasons.
These are all common fears that are included
in the virus programing running in the
background, in the data bank.

Did you learn as a child, if I do this
(whatever this is) I get this? If I don't do
this, there will be punishment and
consequences. Many adults still have this
programing running in the subconscious as
fear. This dense, heavy, disempowering
energy comes from many different sources,
keeping us locked into believing we must
stay within the acceptable structures or we
will suffer.

As the old ways and paradigms collapse,
such as housing, the lifetime jobs with

benefits, disempowering relationships, banking systems, government systems, political systems and many more existing structures, there will be a need for new creative ideas.

A good example is this man that owned his own construction company for building houses, the market collapsed and now he and his crew are building greenhouses. Another example is a person that retired and the social security wasn't meeting her needs so she is creating extra income by selling homemade jelly and pastries. Another example was youth group that needed money and began painting house numbers on the streets.

Maybe it's time to take out the trash or clear old beliefs in order to create a new relationship that is more fulfilling. Each person on this planet has something they like to do that can be shared with others but this requires creating and going beyond the familiar structures.

Playing the blame game, not taking responsibility for our creation and choices is not only common but leads to a dead end street. Negative ongoing conversations can only attract more of the same, creating chaos, drama and disempowering experiences. Wow, such hard words "I screwed that up "and then moving on. Do we really need to add drama and make a mountain out of simple mistakes?

You don't have to believe anything anyone tells you or that is written in this book. Try disengaging from the story, disempowering experiences and see if you have more energy, feel lighter, happier and healthier. Did you know you are your own guru?

Another powerful, simple word that can stop you dead in your tracks is "react". Reacting to others' words and actions is a waste of energy that creates this endless loop going around and around in your head, taking you on the emotional roller coaster.

Playing the game of who is right and who is wrong, develops into many hidden, stuck emotions that get buried if you choose to play. Playing with someone on the emotional roller coaster can drain your energy, disempower you and keep you trapped for days or maybe even years.

Realizing that you are reacting to someone else's' "stuff" which isn't even yours, can stop people from pushing your button. What fun is it to play with someone that doesn't react?

It's amazing how sometimes responding with simple words like "You are absolutely correct" can stop the person that wants you to respond, dead in their tracks. It's kind of funny to watch; they get lost and really don't know what to do if you don't engage with them. You can get creative here and come up with new ways to handle those that like to keep the drama going.

We all know what makes us feel good inside. Maybe it's that walk in nature, quieting the mind, painting a picture, working with wood, building something, doing nothing, going for a swim, cooking yourself something you love, dining out, taking a moment to love yourself, spending quality time with the family, enjoying a conversation with a loved one or just quality time spent with yourself. It doesn't have to be big things.

Taking time to experience small things throughout your day or just spending time alone to get to know you and your deepest self is the best gift you can give yourself. Sorry, taking time for you has to be a commitment on a steady basis to be of any real benefit, just a little time to start with, gradually increasing your special time until it becomes an important part of your lifestyle.

Last but not least, if you state the intention you want to empower yourself and others, focus your attention on that commitment, feed, nourish and live in repetition of empowering yourself, guess what happens?

Yes, empowering others helps empower yourself. One note of caution, empowering others isn't people pleasing, it's seeing their goodness. Maybe it's recognizing their thoughtfulness or a compliment that will raise their energy frequencies. Empowering yourself and others doesn't have to be big things, by paying it forward; this simple tool helps many and creates empowering domino affects. You also get the benefit of raising your energy frequencies, which makes you feel lighter, happier, healthier and can give you a sense of freedom.

That's what it's all about, raising your frequencies to lighter frequencies and clearing, releasing, healing, transmuting those heavy, dense frequencies that weigh us down.

"Only an empowered person can empower others."

ROLE PLAYING

Listed below are some examples of role playing. In the examples I have used names and events which are fictitious. I am using them to help with the awareness and understanding of how role playing is part of our human journey but isn't who we really are. Let's start with the first story of a little girl that loved playing in the imagination.

Once there was a little girl named Joy and she was a beautiful little girl. Joy had golden soft curly hair and the most beautiful blue eyes. Joy loved to play dress up with her mom's clothes. It was so much fun, wearing hi-heels, jewelry, dresses, hats and all the beautiful things. She played with makeup and styled her hair using all the ribbons and bows. Joy received a lot of attention while modeling her different styles and creations.

As Joy grew up she still loved to buy beautiful things, wear beautiful clothing and really loved all the glitz and glamour. She looked at magazines and watched movies of beautiful women.

Joy had fun watching beautiful women express themselves and could feel that beauty within her own self. She liked to express the beauty she felt on the inside by dressing up and this gave her the opportunity to create, using colors, designs, products or anything else that would enhance the role she was playing.

Joy radiated that energy no matter where she went. People enjoyed watching and feeling her energy as she moved with such ease and grace. She attracted beautiful things to herself easily and without effort. Opportunities to model and play the role of a beautiful woman were common experiences. Joy loved it all and totally embraced the feminine aspects of her beauty. She attracted the attention of men, who became dazzled by her beauty. She was so good at playing this role and enjoyed all the people, places and things that went with it.

The opportunity to be a star in the limelight grew day after day, year after year. She was in many movies, modeled and was very busy at being the best that she could be while portraying a life of glitz, glamour and beauty.

As the years went by, Joy grew older, signs of aging set in, which began affecting her opportunities and the role she was playing. Now it was time for Joy to begin playing another role, that role was completed. Wait, this was all Joy knew, she lived it her whole life. What now? Could Joy teach others what she had learned or was there some other way to express herself now?

Joy was never the role she was playing, just experiencing the role of a beautiful woman, playing in the imagination and creating. Will Joy create something else with her skills or will she stay stuck in her past creation?

Maybe Joy is ready to take some time to honor herself in other ways. Maybe she can now spend some time with herself, family and friends, or just enjoy quiet time that she never seemed to have with such a busy, demanding lifestyle.

Now, we will move onto a story about a little boy, doing what he loved, while playing the role of a cowboy. This small boy's name was Sam and he lived on a ranch. Sam was strong, confident and very sure of himself. He had dark hair, big green eyes and a smile that could melt your heart. Sam was filled with happiness and radiated a joyful energy that made it a pleasure to just sit and watch him.

One of Sam's favorite things to do was ride this special pony that his dad gave him as a surprise. Sam was so excited to have his pony and he named the pony, Spirit. Sam and Spirit would go for long rides whenever he got the chance. Sometimes he could barely sleep because he couldn't wait to ride Spirit and be outside on the ranch.

Sam loved getting dressed in his jeans, cowboy boots and of course he had his favorite hat that his mom had given him. Sam saw himself as a cowboy and began playing the role of a cowboy at a very young age. He felt confident, secure and knew in his heart that was all he wanted to be, a cowboy.

As Sam grew older he learned to ride bigger horses and became interested in roping. Sam eventually decided he wanted to experience participating in rodeos. He tried out many different events. He really enjoyed the camaraderie, freedom of the outdoors, traveling, meeting new people and experiencing different places. It was a lifestyle that he absolutely loved and he was playing his favorite role, a cowboy.

Sam's dad and mom were so proud of him. His parents went to watch Sam participate in all the events and rodeos that he had chosen to experience. Sam always enjoyed returning home to good home cooked food, visiting his parents and the ranch. The ranch gave him such an inner peace in his heart that nothing else ever did.

One day Sam saw an ad in the paper, there was to be a bull riding contest and the winner was to receive twenty thousand dollars. Wow, this excited Sam and he could hardly wait to start practicing so he could enter this special event. Sam spent days and months practicing. He was so excited, he loved the challenge and the adrenal rush he got every time he rode the bulls. The feelings of strength and confidence continually grew over time. He just knew he was going to be the winner. Sam could hardly wait!

Sam registered for the bull riding contest which finally came and sure enough with Sam's belief that he could do it, all of his hard work, strength, stamina and courage, Sam was announced the winner.

He was so proud of himself and all his hard work had paid off. He felt for sure he would be happy riding the bulls the rest of his life.

As he grew older, started a family and had a ranch of his own, there was less freedom to participate in the rodeos and he found his interests had changed into breeding and training horses. He always did have a special relationship with horses. Sam really appreciated their stamina, strength and beauty.

Sam changed his role from the daring young rodeo cowboy into a different role and lifestyle that was better suited for his family life, which was also very important to him. Sam didn't come into this life as a cowboy; it's a role he was experiencing, just like experiencing being a husband and father. Sam is still Sam, regardless of the role he choices to play.

Now let's look at a story that can help us better understand the value of the choices we make while choosing to experience a specific role. This story is about playing a role we dislike which can create unhappiness and can ultimately lead to being entangled in many different layered problems.

This story is about a gentleman and his name is Justin. Justin was raised in a very wealthy family. His family was very formal and also very well educated. The entire family was very influential, successful lawyers, doctors, nurses and political figures.

Justin's upbringing was very formal and structured. Some of it was very methodical and there were certain standards expected socially.

Justin's dad and grandfather were very prominent lawyers and Justin was expected to follow the same role as they had. So Justin felt he was doing the right thing when he chose to play the same role and go to school to be a lawyer. He never once asked himself what was best for Justin.

Justin went to presidios schools and although he had to work very hard to get that degree and it was a constant, tremendous struggle, he made it and graduated with honors. There was one problem though; Justin didn't really like what he was doing and wasn't feeling good about himself or what he was doing.

As time went on, Justin tried his best to fit in, meet the expectations and do the best he could at hiding the fact that this role just didn't fit. He really didn't like dressing in the suit and tie or all the structures, paperwork and research that was required. He had watched his grandfather and father represent people for years but he really never had his heart into it.

What would the family say if he didn't want to be a lawyer anymore? What about all that money and time spent on this role that wasn't working? What about carrying on a family tradition? What would he do now? What do you think Justin should do?

As you can see, this chosen role became a very complex issue and now there are many layered problems attached to releasing this particular role. Will Justin follow his heart or stay trapped in the current belief that he needs to be a lawyer?

An important note on roles and titles; there is no title or role that is more important than another. We all came into the world the same way; as an infinite being experiencing life and we will exit the same way, without titles.

Let's take another look at our awareness of role playing. The movies, where actors do just that, play roles, it's part of their life, practicing different roles and playing different characters.

The really good actors have practiced and learned their roles for the movie so well; they are able to actually make you believe they are the character and the role they are playing and it seems so real. It doesn't matter if it's real or not, they become known as that character. In their personal life they may be playing an entirely different role than is being portrayed in the movie.

Maybe a person likes pretending to play many different roles, just for the experience of it or there could be a multitude of other personal reasons why they chose a certain role. As you already know, there are those roles that fit certain characters and those that don't, just like in our own personal lives.

There are those actors that play the bad guy really well and those that save the day. Still other actors portray power, strength and courage in the face of adversity. I often wonder how many actors end up living their personal lives as though they are still acting or playing a role in a movie.

You are the one that has ultimate control of your creation, role and story of your life's journey. Remember, the roles and characters you chose to play aren't who you are; they are created chosen experiences that you have given energy and life to. At any given time you can change your mind. You are an unlimited being with free-will, power to create and the power of choice. You know in your heart which roles you are playing that don't serve you, which ones do and this applies to any area of your life.

What if I don't know what role or roles I want to experience? Use your imagination, create in your mind's eye, pictures of you experiencing the best role you could possibly imagine, add emotions and start pretending that it's yours right now and see what happens. What would it feel like if you were experiencing it now? You already know beliefs are one of the main sources of very powerful energy. Create it in the mind and thus you make it real!

There are many resources available to help you with the manifesting process. Remember to keep it simple and the how is not your job! One more time, the how is not your job!!!

I wonder how much time is being spent throughout the world on giving energy to the things we don't like or even want and wasting energy on reintegrating the past experiences over and over. Wow, that would really make a difference, if we spent more time creating and less time in the endless loop of negativity. Reminder; whatever you are sending energetically to the universe through your thoughts, words or actions, good/bad/right/wrong, will return.

"True wisdom and power lie beyond the illusion of the many different roles and characters we play with."

CHANGE

I have found after many hours and years of research, studying and application, there are many healing techniques, tools and a vast amount of information available. The bottom line seems to be the same message no matter which source you use. Some information is more advanced than others and it depends greatly on where you are in your belief system and what resonates with you personally. Regardless of what the main topics are, it's a time of energy awareness, change and this includes our thoughts, beliefs and creations in one form or another. There are tools available that can help us make the necessary changes globally and personally to be able to move forward with this new energy movement in the evolution process.

As with anything, there are many choices involved in making positive long lasting changes and sometimes this can create a state of overwhelm. Two of the most common questions are "Where do I start?" and "What will work the best for me?"

which can lead to a confusing and frustrating experience. Many have experienced spending money, time and energy on energy tools to help facilitate change without seeing any noticeable difference in their life. Sometimes the tools used, don't do the job and you find the old baggage returning with no apparent change in your life. Reminder; you have to get to the core of the belief, where it first started or it will keep resurfacing in different experiences.

Have you ever gone to a healing workshop, left feeling great for a week or two and returned to the same place you started? Have you ever read a book which inspired you for a while and soon after you fell back into the same old lifestyle and patterns? Did you really take the time to apply the tools for at least twenty one days consistently to create lasting change or are you looking for someone to do it for you or maybe the quick fix that requires no commitment?

Are you still looking outside yourself, going from one thing to the next, next and next, hoping this one will change your life? With so many choices available, it's easy to go from one source to another but believe it or not, you do have all the answers within you. So the best tools would be ones you can do yourself and that will help you access your own answers within your heart and subconscious to create the change you desire. As always, consistency is a must in order to create real change that you would like to experience, otherwise you will end up blowing in the wind, experiencing whatever life throws your way.

Change requires that we let go of our existing current security, undesirable beliefs and leave our comfort zone. Sometimes we will hold onto things regardless of the amount of pain, suffering and hurt it's causing. Why can't we let go? Chances are there is a stuck limiting belief buried or hidden in the subconscious that needs to be cleared or brought into awareness in order to facilitate the desirable change.

The majority of the time the answers are connected to your parents and childhood experiences that are stored in the subconscious. The subconscious is just trying to protect us, even though the experience could be creating a huge amount of pain and suffering. The subconscious will access the past experiences. This doesn't make sense on a conscious level and maybe never will. Remember, you are dealing with very strong beliefs that were possibly formed as a child and have been lived out year after year, experience after experience.

An example of this might be; an abusive relationship that no matter how many times a person has been abused, this person still goes back and experiences more of the same. Another example might be, working eighty hours a week with no time for anything but working, eating and sleeping. Constantly sabotaging yourself could be another example of a hidden belief that is preventing change.

There could be a belief trapped in the subconscious for each of the examples listed above that will keep creating this disharmony, trauma and chaos until it's healed, released and a new one has taken its place.

Everything cleared needs to be replaced with whatever you would prefer to experience (exchanging one belief for another). I have found there is not as much resistance if you say the word exchange for change. Wording is very critical in clearing old beliefs or wanting to change. It can also be that a person is trapped in resistance or fear itself and that needs to be cleared.

Sometimes there are many beliefs connected to the same experience. So any tools that can help change these beliefs will help us move forward, creating something better for ourselves. Even though we want change, we can end up resisting, self-sabotaging and fighting with change. Many times it takes devastation or illness to help us wake up, which will ultimately force us to let go, rather we want to or not.

It is natural for us to resist change because the future and the unknown can be very fearful. Letting go also requires that we trust ourselves and the Divine. We are human and we want to know our future before we make choices, but as you already know, this isn't how life works.

In this time of great change, we are being guided to let go of whatever isn't working or in our best interest. Struggling and working hard to make things happen are going away, these are the old ways that keep creating more of the same. Struggle in this day and age will only get worse, leading to more of that which we are trying to release.

Sometimes it just feels good and makes us feel good to put in a hard day's work and there is nothing wrong with that, but the hard working referred to here is quite different.

One of the main reasons for resisting change is fear. Fear is running rampant throughout the world and individually at this time. Fear has many experiencing feelings of being stuck, trapped and unable to move forward. Would you not agree that in order for change to take place, the existing structures that aren't working need to collapse? This applies to all areas personally and collectively, whether that be housing, money systems, health issues or any other structures that aren't serving the whole or us individually.

Fears are stored in the subconscious and there are several common fears that can keep us feeling disempowered and stuck. Fear of death, pain, consequences, suffering, being hurt, not surviving, loss, not belonging, rejection, abandonment are just a few of the fears that can be hidden and affecting us without our conscious awareness.

I know it doesn't make sense in the conscious mind that we would hold onto a belief that is creating pain, hurt, and suffering, while at the same time, have a fear of suffering if we release the fear.

Remember, you are dealing with the energy trapped from past experiences. The data bank only has the energy of past experiences and beliefs to access, there is no future. So you might say that you are creating your future based on the limited view of past experiences with little or no change.

So now what? We only have one choice that will free us and that is to recognize fear, find any attached beliefs, heal, release and move through it with as much ease and grace as possible in order to experience real change.

Our best tools will be anything that builds self-esteem, self-confidence, self-worth, gives us strength and courage. Please note, it's not about giving fear more power by focusing on it, it's about tools that can help us let go, move through fear, so change can happen.

Many times we are trapped in fear that is not even real and live in that fear day in and out. Fear is also attached to many negative what if questions. Fear is a heavy, dense, dark energy frequency that leads to pain, suffering and eventually can lead to health problems (stored energy in the body). Fear hides out in many different forms.

There are the fears that we are consciously aware of like; fear of bears, fear of water, fear of height and those kinds of fears. Then, there is fears hidden in the subconscious that we have no conscious awareness of. In working with many people and in my research, there are several other kinds of fears that come as a surprise to many. Some of these are; fear of loss, fear of success (yes, this is correct), fear of failure, fear of not being enough or good enough, fear of losing weight, fear of having money, fear of not belonging and many, many more.

The bottom line, fear is a big powerful word that needs our attention individually and collectively in order to create positive change. This is no surprise to most but what many don't realize, if you focus your intention and attention on building your self-confidence, self-esteem and self-love, this will help you recognize fear, feel it, disclaim it and release it. Ask for help from Source to give you courage, strength and the best way to release fear with ease and grace, so that you may experience the change you would like to experience.

I would also question any healing technique that claims to clear fear in one clearing because it's so individualized. Yes, there are some standards that are similar in many but we each have our own story and experiences.

An example of this might be fear of money. Money has many different fears attached to it energetically. Clearing a fear of not having money, probably won't create much change in your financial picture because of all the different layers and dynamics that are intertwined with the energy of money.

Let's take a look at a few other areas where we have been affected by change. Probably one of the most profound changes that has affected the world collectively and individually on all levels is the computer technology. That technology is still changing our lives drastically in several different areas.

Another change that has been affecting our lives, the birth of extended warranties. Is a good change, buying something new, with an extended warranty, so we won't have to live in fear of it breaking down? Could we have prevented the extended warranty saga from even happening so we wouldn't have to live in fear of not having warranties? Can we stop the insanity of changes that keep us locked in fear?

We are all seeing some pretty major changes connected to Mother Earth. Mother Earth has always been changing and will continue to change. Our weather patterns are changing quite drastically in some places.

Is Mother Earth forcing us to make substantial changes that can help everyone? Is there a drastic need for change connected to Mother Earth or will fear keep us held hostage?

If you look at every area that needs change, I think it would be fair to say, you could probably find fear at the base of anything that isn't working and needs to be changed.

So you see when you look at the word "change", its power is all around us and has a profound affect in every area of our personal lives and collectively. Because there are so many changes necessary at this time, it's important that we start making positive changes to empower ourselves in order to move forward.

As long as we remain in fear of change there will be no positive change and living in fear will lead to more of the same (like attracts like). We may not be able to save the world or solve the problems of the world by ourselves but if each of us move through our own personal fears, that energy resonates to others, family, friends, loved ones and helps in the creation of a better world.

Caution should be taken in the choices we make connected to change. Are we looking outside of ourselves for change in hopes that it will change what we are feeling or experiencing inside?

As we are all very well aware of, sometimes the grass looks greener on the other side. Is it really time for a change in a relationship or does the relationship with ourselves need to change? Are we thinking, if only this person, place or thing would change, my life would be better? Are some changes even necessary or does my perception or belief need to change? We need to start asking more valuable deeper questions.

So, the bottom line, change is inevitable in our individual lives and globally. Many of us have already lived through many changes and I'm sure we will all live through many more changes in our lifetime, some for the better and some not so good. By bringing our awareness, intention and attention to making changes that are necessary, we can learn to flow with life, rather than the alternative choice of living in fear, swimming upstream against the flow, resisting change, creating chaos, trauma and dysfunction.

Maybe healing a belief or releasing a current false belief could make change flow smoother and easier. We are human though, so many of us do have a belief, if we struggle long enough and work hard enough that we can make whatever it is work! Once again, in order to live our dreams, create the life we desire and move forward, we must let go and welcome change as a good thing!!!

"Change is inevitable, nothing stays the same."

SUMMARY

As I began my research, my main purpose was to understand what the majority of people from all walks of life were experiencing at this time, their stories. I wanted to know why so many people were suffering in various ways, why there was so much stress (buzzword), fear and dysfunction in the world today. I wanted to know why so many of our young people are committing suicide, involved in mass violent acts, being drugged and tagged. I also wanted to know what if anything, all this had to do with energy and if there were things that could help people, our young people and our children to experience an easier, better quality of life without all the pain, struggle and suffering.

My research has taken me to many different sources and through a multitude of variables. At the base of the research; our attachment to experiences, beliefs and emotions were the main sources of distress.

I also included in this book other contributing factors that I felt were important. The information in this book includes many years of research, studying and listening to many, many stories. Although everyone has their own story, there are many underlying similarities.

While on this path; I found how energy work, understanding, awareness were crucial and at the core of everything. We can name it, tag it, define it and do whatever else we would like but we are energy beings experiencing life on earth at this time. While experiencing life, we are creating our experiences as we learn to expand our consciousness. With our gift of free will, we can choose whatever we want.

We are curious beings with a natural sense of wanting to create. One of the main sources of pain, hurt and struggle is getting trapped in emotional attachments to those experiences, people, places and things. Living in the past but faced with the duality of wanting to move forward.

Another contributing factor is fear; it has the ability to stop us dead in our tracks, frozen in time. There is a mass of consciousness trapped, living in fear at this time, feeling stuck, helpless and victimized.

I also found there is a large mass of people, young people and children with little or no self-confidence, self-esteem, lack of self-worth and self-love. Could the base of this be that we have become a service oriented society, living in the Information Age with little or no self-awareness? Have we as a society, became trapped in tunnel vision, doing steps one through ten, locked in the survival mode? What will it take to break us free? Does it have to be devastation before we can make changes or is a deeper understanding needed beyond all the stories?

There are many health issues, relationship problems, money problems and many are lost in the world of outside attachment, searching for help in experiencing a happier, healthier, and more satisfying life on all levels. Many are searching for the very basics of life, feeling loved, appreciated, wanted and needed.

Your best choices would be to use tools that can help you find this truth on the inside, feel it, experience it in the now, then those desires will be fulfilled from the outside world. Reminder; it's all about energy, like attracts like. In order for changes to be more than just a temporary fleeting moment in time, it will always be an inside job first, before you notice any substantial long term changes.

You are the only one that knows what is best for you and can make any changes in your life. There is no way around taking responsibility for your life. You are the only one that has control over your mind.

Really understanding and experiencing on a very deep level the reality that we are powerful beings beyond our stories can change our lives drastically and empower us.

Who created your story? Do you realize how much courage and strength that it took to create your story in the first place? Learning to use the imagination with direction, focus and intention is a key to unlocking the door to the infinite being you are and claiming our "I AM" can facilitate that into reality. Whatever we chose to play with or imagine, good or bad, the law of attraction is truth and that choice will grow whether we are aware or not.

The world is like a giant puzzle, each one of us is an important part of that puzzle and the Divine plan otherwise we would not be here. It's our responsibility, as the co-creators to use our power of free will to make wise choices that empower us individually and also serve for the good of all.

Life is filled with choices; you can be in a constant state of struggle, playing the role of victim, living in fear or anything else you choose. There would be no purpose to be on Earth at this time if the Divine didn't think you had some special gift that could be shared to help humanity in the evolution process.

Here is some information that might help you know how special you are; out of billions of people living on earth at this time and billions before us, there is only one of you, unless you are an identical twin. Amongst your many attributes, there is no one that has your unique brain, your imagination, creativity, gifts, fingerprints, expressions, DNA or dreams.

It's up to each one of us individually, to know ourselves, realize our gifts, share, empower ourselves, take action and stop being controlled by outside influences. Outside influences just keep us out of balance, out of harmony, off track, distracted, feeling unfulfilled and lost in the busyness of life, in a state of constant turmoil, drama and chaos of the outside world.

You will find some tools listed at the back of this book to help you get started on your path of energy awareness. This list is by no means even a fraction of the resources available or that I studied, researched and utilized.

Through research, study, trial and error, I have created my own methods of clearing away stuck energy, beliefs and experiences. I have also been blessed with the ability to help people find their truth, while facilitating and sharing messages from source.

Trust that you will be guided to whatever you need and ask the powers above to lead you to whatever will serve you at this time. In case you didn't know, you must ask for help because of your gift of free will. After you ask, please be sure and let go of how you think your answers should come.

Remember, your resources are limited compared to the powers above.

May the sun shine upon your path, filling your hearts and homes with love, laughter, joy and light. May you come to know your truth, love yourself and share your light with the world. May the white light always surround and protect you as you journey inward, raising energy consciousness, creating a better world for the good of all.

Love, Light and Blessings, Shirley

TOOLS

COLOUR ENERGY

SOUND

ARMOTHERAPHY

HYPNOTHERAPHY

ENERGY TESTING

COLOUR ENERGY

Have you ever thought about how colours affect you? Colour energy is one of our best sources for raising our energy frequencies and lifting our spirit. Whether we are aware of it or not, colour has energy frequencies that affect our moods, energy and health. Colour is good and the more the better!

Take a moment and think about going to the fair. The majority of people going to a fair will have smiles on their faces and in their hearts. Many are filled with laughter, joy and happiness while in this experience. Most are feeling lighter, all of the worries and fears lift, if only for a short time. We already have this energy inside of us and this experience reminds us of those higher frequencies that vibrate within our being.

Another good example of the effects of lights, colour and music can be found in Las Vegas, Nevada. One of the fascinating things to do in Las Vegas is to watch people when they first arrive. For the first few days they become mesmerized by all the lights and colours. For a while they are just fascinated by the energy that surrounds them. These energy frequencies are being felt and recognized internally with or without awareness. We are light beings, even though we are living in a human body. If you go to Fremont street where the sixties music is playing, the lights are flashing and the colours are bountiful, you will see people as they dance, sing and play with the lights, colour and music. It doesn't seem to make any difference if they are children or older, it has the same effect on the majority.

Hawaii is another great place to get a mega dose of colour energy and all of your senses will awaken as you visit. All the majestic colours seem to remind us of our need to feed our spirits, or you might say to lighten up.

Why is it that we feel so well, at peace when experiencing the natural wonders of the ocean, at the beach, walking in the forest and in nature's beauty? All of our senses, on a very deep level become alive and expand to a deeper state of awareness as we experience Mother Earths' gifts.

There are many different cultures and parts of the world that use colour in abundance. The men, women and children wear the different colours, their food is very colourful, their products and décor is bright, cheery and uplifting. Many are drawn to experience vacations in these colourful places. Have you ever wondered why, in the United States that the colours are suppressed in many areas except for children and young people?

Why is this? We are light energy beings and we are automatically drawn to colour and lights. The fourth of July is another example of lights and colour.

Again, the energy vibrations and frequencies come from within and are activated by outside stimuli. What do I mean by this? It's important to realize that it doesn't mean that we need to go places to stimulate those energy frequencies, which already exist within ourselves. Kind of like the syndrome; I will be happy when I get this or I go here.

Even though there are many beautiful places to visit that are very colourful, we don' have to go anywhere. We are powerful beings that have the ability to create right where we are in our minds. So for those that can't visit these beautiful places in person, we can still visualize colour, use it in our décor, focus on it, experience it and still have the healing affects, no matter where we are and what we are doing. Who knows, you might even get to experience more colourful experiences, like attracts like!

There are many different resources, data and case studies available for those wanting to expand their awareness of the power of colour.

There are also many different healing resources available that use colour energy in energy work. I have researched, utilized and studied many different forms of healing with colour but have chosen to list only a few.

Colour Energy is a company that has a full line of products that can be very beneficial in working with colour. This company's main focus is on colour energy and its affects. I have personally used many of their products and find them to have excellent quality. This company is mainly for retailers or people with a business.

Colour Energy is a book written by Inger Naess. She has listed in a very colourful, comprehensive book the many different aspects connected to colour. It's a good book that is simple, easy and a great reference book to have in your personal library.

<u>Colors & Numbers</u> by Louise L. Hay is a very simple but powerful book. For those of you that aren't familiar with Louise, she has helped and touched the lives of many people in her healing work.

<u>The Healing Power of Color</u> is a book by Betty Wood, which has been around for a long time. Betty helps us understand how to use color to improve our mental, physical and spiritual well-being.

You might want to check out these resources and have fun playing with color to make your life more colourful! Why not pick a colour and play with it for a week or so and see what happens? Sounds to simple, right? Simple is good!

SOUND

Ancient wisdom of sound healing is now main stream and there are various tools available that can be used easily, quickly and effectively. Modern science now has equipment that can measure and validate the effects of using sound vibration for energy healing in various forms. There is a vast amount of scientific research, evidence, studies and data available for those interested in validation of sound healing proof that sound does, in fact, affect us and can have healing benefits. Modern technology has made it incredibly easy to integrate the healing benefits of sound into our lifestyle.

Some sound vibrations can be used to experience raising our frequencies, while other frequencies and vibrations can create healing in the human body on a deep level. There are even specific sounds for specific organs.

There are sounds or music mixed with subliminal messages that can change those destructive beliefs stored in the subconscious even while sleeping. How does it get any easier than that?

I am referring to music and sounds that actually resonate with our energetic body, not white noise. Yes, we have our favorite songs and music which lifts our spirits and helps us produce feel good chemicals in our body but that isn't the same as the vibrations from the various sound forms such as: singing bowls, ancient sounds, chanting, didgeridoo, drumming, sounds for meditation, tuning forks and many other methods of healing with sound.

Of course, some of the best sources of sound are in nature which can bring us peace, serenity, balance and healing. Even in nature though, some people get irritated at the sound of birds, raging water, turbulence of the ocean waves and sometimes the silence of nature or the serenity in the desert can make some uneasy because they are accustomed to white noise and it's very uncomfortable to have it quiet.

Some of the newer sources of sound therapy would be specific vibrations such as; solfeggio frequencies, music and sound designed to reach induced trance states, binaural rhythms, ultrasound, brainwave synchronization, and cymatics are just a few of the possibilities that can help to reach a deeper state of consciousness.

The art of sound healing used consistently can create stress reduction, peaceful mind states, produce healthy chemicals in the body, facilitate emotional healing, can help release blocked energy, facilitate healing after illness, reduce the effects of traumas which were caused by invasive medical treatments, increase vital energy flow, increase creativity, increase your intuition, induce harmony to your entire being, clear a busy mind, help release anxiety and these are only a few of the benefits. There are very few tools that can be used so easily and have such great health benefits.

By using specific frequencies, waves of energy or vibrations, it's possible to experience profound energy changes and awareness within. Regardless of what source you choose, just a few minutes a day of taking time for you, can create a greater state of health mentally, emotionally, physically, spiritually and be very therapeutic.

A word of caution on using sound for healing: take some uninterrupted time to listen and feel your body as you listen to the chosen product, if it doesn't feel good, stop! Some of the sound therapy has poor quality because of equipment or poor recording devices. An example of this might be 532 Hz, known for the frequencies connected to love, but the frequency might not be of quality. You know you better than anyone else, if everyone is listening to this frequency and it doesn't resonate with you, that is OK!

I am so grateful for those individuals that have dedicated their life to sound healing, studying the effects and benefits of sound energetic forms . This also helps us understand how we too can utilize the different forms of sound energy healing to help ourselves, friends, family and raise our energy levels to a healthier level. Listed below are three of the most popular sound healing creators.

Mark Romero

"Mark educates people worldwide on the science of energy as it relates to human functioning and empowers them with music."

Jim Oliver

"Jim is a sensitive and dynamic musician and composer of more than 3500 hours of transformational healing music."

Jonathan Goldman

"Jonathan is an author, musician and teacher in the fields of harmonics and sound healing. In 2011, he was listed by the Watkins Review as one of the 100 most spiritually influential people of the world."

AROMATHERAPY

Aromatherapy can help clear your home of negative energy, raise energy frequencies, create a wellness feeling, calm the mind and body, clear confusion, helps with scattered energy, clear out sick, stagnant, stale energy and those are only a few examples of the many benefits of essential oil.

Using essential oil is effective, simple, easy, quick and works for those people on the go. You might try boiling some water, adding a few drops of essential oil to the water, enjoy the experience and effects, as your senses react to such subtle but powerful energy. You can put some drops in your bath, place a few drops on your pulse points or on your pillow. Experience it for yourself how these simple drops can and do affect your energy.

Your senses can tell the difference between synthetic oils and natural oils. You may experience health issues if using synthetic oils.

Listed below are a few helpful resources for using aromatherapy.

Aromatherapy 101
    Karen Downes

Young Living Essential Oils

Essential Oils That Build Natural Defenses
    Dr. William H. Lee with Greg Holt

Aromahealth Texas
    Dr. Judy Griffin, PhD

HYPNOTHERAPY

This healing art is used to reach a very deep relaxing state of consciousness that can help you get beyond the mind chatter into a much more sacred space within. I call it a healing art because it takes a qualified, skilled person to be able to help people get beyond their everyday lives, the roles they play and the logical mind.

There are many different tools a hypnotherapist can use to help relax your body and mind. Some might use very relaxing scripts, while others may use a combination of special music, sounds, aromatherapy and their voice. Each hypnotherapist has their own style, techniques and methods for inducing altered consciousness states. You may want to try out more than one hypnotherapist before you decide which one resonates with you the best.

Hypnotherapy is a direct line of access to the

subconscious mind (data bank). Why would you want to access the subconscious? Healing, answers and limiting beliefs reside in this area. It can be very beneficial to those that are experiencing habitual patterns of attracting bad relationships, money problems, self-sabotage, health issues, fears, phobias, abuse issues, weight issues or any other area that is attracting continuous negative experiences.

Remember, you have to get to the core of any issue before you can really heal. The logical mind or will power has little or no power in healing core issues. Many that have tried to heal from the logical mind, still end up re-experiencing that which they thought was healed and released. Even those that thought they had forgiven can find old wounds or similar experiences reappearing. Hypnotherapy will take you to the core issues, the current problem or issue isn't where the real problem lies, it's only a layer.

There are many negative, limiting beliefs connected to hypnotherapy but usually the core is based on fear. Some of these fears are; fear of losing control, fear of what will happen while in this state of consciousness, fear of the hypnotherapist, fear of doing something wrong, fear of something bad happening, fear of exposing deep secrets, and the list goes on and on. None of these fears are truth, you will be safe, aware and in control! If you can drop all the fears, use the power of intention, release and let go while experiencing this peaceful, relaxing state, I think you will be pleasantly surprised at the results and the power of this healing art in all areas of your life. They even us hypnotherapy in hospitals before and after surgery for quicker and healthier recovery

If you have tried hypnotherapy before and nothing happened, please try again, again and again until you experience this healing art. Maybe you weren't ready or the fear was so strong you wouldn't allow yourself this experience. This healing art is one of the best healing tools for those deep seated issues. It might take more than one session to experience the healing benefits but your rewards can be profound.

There is plenty of information available on hypnotherapy and different states of consciousness. It has been around for a very long time and this art has been perfected over the years. What have you got to lose? Living a life of struggle, pain and hurt is no longer necessary or honorable. Maybe it would be a good idea to learn self-hypnosis.

I have not listed any sources because I feel like this is a very personalized area. Finding someone you trust and resonate with is very important when doing this type of work.

ENERGY TESTING

There are many different techniques and tools available for testing energy. Remember, everything is energy. Some samples of common terminology for testing energy that you may or may not be familiar with are; muscle testing, kinesiology, pendulum testing or water witching. The various tools and methods used for testing energy can help you quickly and easily find your own personal answers. Energy testing can also save you a lot of money and help you make better choices. You can use energy testing in all areas of your life and it will help take a lot of the guess work out of making choices.

I have personally used the pendulum for about forty years. There are no words to describe all the benefits that I have experienced, especially in health, not only for myself but for my family, friends and others. I chose the pendulum because I wanted to be able to do it myself and have one hand free. I am so grateful for having this form of energy testing in my life. It has served me well! I have found this form of energy testing to be accurate if I pay close attention to what I am asking and get out of my own way.

One of the biggest challenges in energy testing is asking clear focused questions. When using any form of testing it's necessary to learn what words to use to get accurate answers, you can change one word and it makes all the difference in the world. It takes time, consistent practice and trust in yourself.

Once you expand the mind, get beyond the how come, what for, questioning with the logical mind whether it really works, criticism of others, doubt, fear of what others will think, it can and will open a whole new paradigm of working with energy and energy awareness. Why not take some time to do some research on the benefits of energy testing and find which energy testing method will meet your needs?

RESOURCES

MOVIES

SPEAKERS/INTERVIEWERS

HEALING MODALITIES

BOOKS

BODY HEALING

SCIENTIFIC DATA

QUANTUM HEALERS

REMOTE HEALERS

MOVIES

Of course we all have our favorite movies which inspire us, lift our spirits, make us laugh and help us to experience our emotions in their deepest most innocent state. Here is a listing of a few movies that expand the consciousness beyond the normal, help in understanding some of the deeper more profound intricacies of the human experience and expand your energy awareness. Movies like these inspire us to go beyond the mundane to experience our unlimited potential, possibilities and miracles beyond what the logical mind can possibly perceive.

The Secret
Avatar
The Matrix
What the Bleep!? Down the
    Rabbit Hole

I also want to bring special attention to Dan Milan's movie **"The Peaceful Warrior"**. It's an older movie that was way before it's time. This movie gives us a better understanding of the effects of energy, how we are affected by it and helps us understand how to create a deeper more meaningful life. You may need to watch this movie several times to be able to really experience the full message. There are numerous words of wisdom portrayed in this movie that can be integrated into our own personal lives.

SPEAKERS/ INTERVIEWERS

Listening to speakers and interviews online can help us with motivation, inspire us to take action, give us new tools that can help us personally, give us tools to heal old wounds, give us new beliefs, help us to let go of what is not serving us, open our minds to new possibilities, hear other peoples' stories that are similar and the list goes on and on. These speakers and guests help like-minded people come together to create a large community of people from around the world sharing experiences, knowledge healing tools and global consciousness. All of the speakers I am aware of offer some free resources for those in need and if you don't own a computer, the library is a great source for listening to speakers and their guests.

Research is an important part of my work and it's because of this, I have listened to several broadcasting shows online, over many years. My main focus has been to find out what the majority of people around the world are experiencing at this time and studying healing tools available that can help people make changes in their own personal lives to experience a better, more rewarding and fulfilling life.

Modern technology has made it possible for energy understanding and awareness to reach the masses. You can experience energy shifts just by listening to the broadcasts. Sometimes the energy shifts are significant, sometimes you might not feel anything and that is OK. Maybe the energy shifts will be on a deep cellular level and later you will have the "ah ha" moment or maybe it will be information that can be used to help a friend, family member or yourself later on. I am personally grateful for their dedication, commitment and intention to help enlighten the lives of many.

Even though I am only including a few of the broadcasters in my list, there are many. Remember energy follows thoughts so you can get clear, state your intention, focus your attention on what you would like to experience and you will be lead to what will resonate with you.

Healing With the Masters
Jennifer Mclean

You Wealth Revolution
Darius M. Barazandeh

Wellness Revolution
Adoley Odunton

New Realities
Alan Steinfeld

Rainmaking Time
Kim Greenhouse

The Juicy Living Tour
Lilou Mace

RADIO BROADCASTING

NEWS FOR THE SOUL

HAY HOUSE RADIO

THINKING ALLOWED

JUST ENERGY RADIO

COAST TO COAST

AWAKENING ZONE

SHEILA GALE

HEALING MODALITIES

There are more forms of mind, body healing methods and mind, body, soul integration available now than has ever been in my lifetime or maybe any lifetime. A large part of the energy healing movement has been one of the gifts that the internet has made possible. The massive amounts of information available on energy awareness and healing can be a bit overwhelming in making the best choice that will personally serve you.

Some of the main sources of energy healing in the past were; meditation, massage, hypnotherapy, reiki, yoga, acupressure, acupuncture NLP (Neuro Linguistic Programing). These practices are still valuable but we are now learning that we must include the mind, beliefs and emotions in the healing processes and this is our own personal responsibility.

There is much controversy over the movie "The Secret" but if this movie hadn't become main stream, I really don't think energy awareness would be where it is today. I am personally grateful for the movie expanding my consciousness, reminding me that I am a powerful unlimited being, helping me understand that my thoughts are my responsibility, teaching me that it is possible to create dreams and experiences.

Wow, I wonder how many lives have been touched by understanding the "Law of Attraction". Regardless of all the criticism and so called missing pieces, it did wake many people up, realizing our thoughts and emotions are energy in motion that are affecting us continually. How could this one movie possibly include all of our own personal stories, emotions and beliefs or be responsible for fixing our lives?

As energy awareness becomes more main stream, people are starting to use specialized formats for their particular area of expertise. In your search, one of the best guides would be to follow "Simple is Good". If there are too many procedures, steps and the healing modality is too complex, it can be very hard to follow through with a commitment and consistency. Sometimes it's hard to believe, if it's too simple it will not work. Many are accustomed to making everything difficult or struggling as a way of life, thinking it's noble and wanting everything to be a challenge to be conquered. Of course much of this is done without conscious awareness. Challenges have their place but don't have to be a consistent factor in everything we do. The old way of struggle or making everything difficult will only produce more of the same in the world of energy awareness.

We all live in a very busy world and many have gotten use to a very fast paced lifestyle. This is nothing we don't already know but as long as we are consistently busy or preoccupied with "stuff" outside ourselves, we will remain in a constant search leading to an unfulfilled life. This is another reason healing techniques and tools need to be simple, easy, fast and can be used anytime and anywhere. How can we ever know ourselves, if we are constantly stimulated by outside sources? Are there children that are so consistently stimulated by outside sources that they need to be constantly entertained or have to have the latest this or that to entertain them?

Please don't under estimate the power or speed at which the mind works, it's incredible. Take a moment now to think about this concept. Have you ever had a thought and it very quickly grew into a whole entourage of other thoughts until a whole story with attached emotions was created, positive or negative, in a matter of seconds or minutes? This is when we need fast, simple and effective tools or methods. Maybe just a simple word like "stop" will calm the chatter, illusions and the ride on the emotional roller coaster.

A word of caution; wording is critical. A few examples of this are; embarrassment is not the same as humiliation, clearing resentment when it's really a feeling of being left out, wounded energy is different than hurt, self-sabotage is different than self-abuse and so on. I have seen many people trying to clear words, energy and experiences with energy that doesn't resonate with them personally. This can create frustration and cause feelings of failure. The majority of energy healing needs will be found in the emotional field and belief system before there will be any noticeable difference in health, relationships or in any other areas.

These are just a few of the energy healing methods which I found to be very helpful in my research connected to healing energy tools. Included are some of the best healing methods and information, teachings and each one has their benefits. One that is not as well-known as the others is T.A.T (Tapas Acupressure Technique) but I had some of my greatest breakthroughs using this healing method. EFT (Emotional Freedom Technique/Tapping) is one of the most popular and biggest healing method that I know of at this time.

Since I have worked with the different healing techniques, I have created my own simple, easy, fast methods for clearing energy. There are many techniques that don't get to the core, are too long and take too much time. Many that have worked very hard and spent many hours clearing are finding old issues resurfacing. There are various reasons for this happening but muscle testing is an extremely valuable tool for testing the effectiveness of energy clearing, especially for quantum healings.

A word of caution for those that are spending the majority of their time clearing; it is better to have a balance and spend the majority of time in creating and playing with the imagination.

The Emotion Code
Dr. Bradley Nelson

The Tapping Cure
Roberta Temes, PhD

Freedom Is
Brandon Bays

The Journey
Brandon Bays

The Healing Code
Alex Lloyd PhD, ND
Ben Johnson, MD, DO, NMD

The Tapas Acupressure Technique
Tapas Fleming

Tessera Method
Adam King

Access Consciousness
Gary Douglas

Heart Math
Howard Martin

Silva Method
    Laura Silvia

You Can Heal Your Life
    Louise L. Hay

**Imagery for Healing, Knowledge and
    Power**
    William Fezler, PhD

Ho'oponopono
    Dr. Hew Len

Ask and Receive
    Sandi Radomski and Tom Altaffer

BOOKS

There are many books that can help inspire us, facilitate a greater understanding of energy awareness or be that helping hand when needed. Some of the authors have been around for a long time and are well known. Many others are simply sharing their stories and experiences in hope of helping others. I have found that most people are naturally drawn to the book they need, at the time, depending on where they are in their personal journey. There are no coincidences. Listed below are a few you may or may not be aware of.

Dying To Be Me
    Anita Moorjanio
Your Body Doesn't Lie
    John Diamond, M.D.
Sacred Signs
    Adrian Calabrese, PhD
The Power Of Now
    Eckhart Tolle
The Art of True Healing
    Israel Regardie

The Magical Path
     Marc Allen
Water
     Dr. Emoto
What Do You Mean The Third Dimension is Going Away?
     Jim Self and Roxane Burnett
How to Think like Leonardo da Vinci
     Michael J. Gelb
Freedom & resolve (The Living Edge Of Surrender)
     Gangaji
Silent Power
     Stuart Wilde
Miracles
     Stuart Wilde
Ageless Body, Timeless Mind
     Deepak Chopra M.D.
The Answer is Simple/Love Yourself Live your Spirit!
     Sonia Choquette
The New Psycho-Cybernetics
     Maxwell Maltz, M.D.,F.I.C.S.
     (edited & updated by Dan S. Kennedy)

BODY HEALING

There are many different teachings and various forms available for working directly with the body to facilitate healing energy and increase vital energy flow. Below are just a few body healing methods that have been very beneficial for those seeking help with physical ailments.

Please remember that it's also important to integrate the healing on all levels and this includes the mind, beliefs, emotions, thoughts, etc. The head isn't separate from the body, although many tend to live in their heads the majority of the time.

The Touch of Healing
        Alice Burmeister with Tom Monte
Energy Medicine with/ Donna Eden
Spring Forest QiGong/ Chunyi Lin
Mudras/ Gertrud Hirschi
Kundalini Yoga/ Gaiam/Gurmukh
Five Rites

SCIENTIFIC DATA

The individuals I have listed below can give us a better understanding of energy on a deeper, more scientific level. Through their many hours of studying, research and application, they have scientifically proven many energy related theories.

Gregg Braden "(researcher, author and speaker) He is internationally renowned as a pioneer in bridging science, ancient wisdom and the real world".

Dr. Bruce Lipton "(stem cell biologist, author, keynote speaker) He is recognized internationally as a leader bridging science and spirituality".

Dr. Joe Dispenza "(neuroscientist, chiropractor, lecturer, author) Known for creating a bridge between true human potential and the latest scientific theories of neuroplasticity".

QUANTUM HEALERS
REMOTE HEALERS

Quantum healers (facilitators) are those individuals that work with mass consciousness, groups of people at the same time and can also facilitate long distance healing. They also can work with clearing many people at the same time, which have similar disempowering beliefs and stuck energy. They clear energy in workshops, remotely and some do individual clearings. They each have their own methods and style for moving mass consciousness to a more empowering level.

Panache Desai
Kenji Kumara
Jo Dunning
Rikka Zimmerman
Dain Heer

For many years people had to seek out one on one healers. With the new energy movement, came the ability for several healers to be able to work with healing energies remotely (healing across the miles).

As always, each healer utilizes their own unique gifts for clearing energy or facilitating healing energy to the person in need. Some energy healers also work with animals. These remote healers can be booked for many months ahead.

You can also find remote healers on talk or radio shows. Effective remote healing is a very individualized process and your success with this method greatly depends upon your belief system.

Rudy Hunter
Susan Shumsky
Emanuel Dagher
Christie Marie Sheldon
Mashhur Anam

The truth we seek is within ourselves. We do have everything we need but sometimes these outside sources can help us move beyond our limited perceptions, beliefs and stories to experience higher energy frequencies more consistently.